In Search Of Big Fish

An Angler's Memoirs

The serious and humorous recollections of over 40 years of rock and surf fishing in South Africa and Australia.

In Search of Big Fish

An Angler's Memoirs

First Printing December, 2014

ISBN: 978-0-9942171-1-0

Published by The Mickie Dalton Foundation
Kempsey, NSW
Australia

www.mickiedaltonfoundation.com

Contents

Part Three: On Fishing From The Rocks

Chapter 12

Some suggestions for staying alive on the rocks while fishing

Chapter 13

Some considerations and methods that could help to ensure that big fish are landed successfully

Chapter 14

A few final words

Acknowledgements

My first words of gratitude go to Whomever is responsible for the fact that there are oceans full of fish and other fascinating animals. Secondly, I am deeply indebted to the late Professors JLB and MM Smith of the JLB Smith Institute of Ichthyology in South Africa, who inspired me so much in my younger years.

To my wife Judy, for understanding my passion for fishing and encouraging me to do so, for her advice on the content of this book, and for proofreading the manuscript, my heartfelt gratitude. My warm thanks to Deb Williams for her numerous good suggestions and for proofreading the manuscript at least twice.

Thanks also to Ray Good of South West Rocks, a very dedicated angler from whom I learned to say "I *NEED* to go fishing!" (I will never just 'want' to go fishing again.)

Finally, my most sincere thanks to Michael Davies of the Mickie Dalton Foundation, Kempsey, New South Wales, Australia, who, after discovering this manuscript, offered to undertake the substantial task of publication. How to properly thank Michael for his remarkable generosity with both time and very considerable skill is still eluding me. I am aware of how much assistance he has rendered to other authors as well, and would like to take this opportunity to thank him most warmly on behalf of us all.

Introduction:

A Few Bits and Pieces, and Some Serious Stuff Up Front

I originally considered calling this book *'My Brilliant Fishing Career'* after the Australian film *'My Brilliant Career'*. However that presented a problem – it was to be a book based on fact, and in the strictest sense (or any other sense for that matter) my fishing activities have not actually produced an income. Nope! In fact no amount of fiddling with the numbers could produce a *cost* of less than about $500 per kilogram of fish caught – and that was with some cheating. Not even to *my* retarded business mind could this be construed as a profitable activity. But, at least the rest of the name would have been true – the 'fishing' and the 'brilliant' are correct.

'Brilliant' ??? Oh hell yeah! It's been brilliant for sure. In the sense of enjoyable, that is. After all, who *wouldn't* want to crawl out of bed at 4.00 a.m. in the chilly dark of winter, pull on yesterday's cold, damp (and smelly) fishing clothes; step from a rain-soaked tent into a slush of mud and wet grass with hands stinging from infected cuts, fin-spine holes and hook punctures; grope in the blackness to gather up a bunch of fishing rods ("OWWW, *damn*, didn't I take the hooks off last night!?") and a soggy fishing bag ("Oh *bloody* hell, I left the bait in there *again* – PHEEWWW, what a stink!"); slip/slide down the mountain-side and stagger/stumble over boggy streams and

rocky outcrops for thirty minutes to get to the sacred fishing spot?

(Well, who wouldn't want to...?)

Actually, this was not originally intended to be an amusing account, but uninvited humour kept creeping in. *Hours* were spent trying to eliminate funny stuff from what was meant to be a serious document, but it was impossible, so I gave up in the end. (Nor was it possible but for the briefest moments to remove my tongue fully from my cheek.) Fishing and humour are two inseparable creations, proving not only that there *is* a God, but that He has a lively, if somewhat twisted sense of humour. Though not as twisted as my own, of course.

However the book *is* factual – all of the fish described are actual captures, with photographs to verify this. Similarly, the humorous events also actually took place, though the stories attached to a few of the photographs are a little tongue in cheek.

Fishing, despite being liberally infused with humour, is also a deeply serious matter – that is perhaps its greatest beauty. It offers the opportunity for both laughter *and* a fulfilment of the human soul to depths that have to be experienced to be believed. And it doesn't stop there! It can work wonders for the ego too!

When it comes to the matter of humorous and serious, the two can overlap. That means that something that appears humorous may also be serious and it pays to be aware. It is less serious if the *humorous* side of something

2

serious is missed! A waste, but not serious. For example, it pays not to cut one's bait on a rocky area that may later be needed for sitting on. This may seem trivial, but if rocky places that reasonably accommodate the shape of one's posterior (and these are very rare) are needed for sitting on, it is better if they are not covered with bait cuttings. Even washing them will render them wet and unusable for some time. These are important rock fishing matters.

Getting back to the more serious, the unavoidable fun and funny events recounted here are only light dots on a far deeper and more mysterious code of being that is indelibly embedded in my own psyche, and in those of millions of others like me. It is as enduring as a leopard's spots... I passionately love the oceans and the life in them – there is some special kind of primordial mystery and magic about them. The fact that we kill and eat our catches does not contradict this. It has nothing to do with it. Life has supported Life at its own expense for aeons. That is its very nature. A fluctuating, pulsating continuity with populations of living organisms arising, flourishing and eventually disappearing.

On the other hand I am vehemently opposed to unnecessary killing or wilful cruelty, and especially to over-fishing. To over-exploit is not merely short-sighted – it is totally blind and stupid. But, incredibly, it continues to happen even in this day and age despite our increasingly comprehensive knowledge and understanding of fish stocks. Consider international commercial fishing trends. Stocks are often fished to the edge of extinction before measures are taken to protect them – frequently against violent protests. Imagine how much more we could regularly harvest, if, instead of persisting in harvesting the annual yield from a depleted stock consisting of 10 or 20% of the original numbers, we allowed these to *fully* recover, and then harvested sustainably from the full stock. Hmmm, oh well, I suppose that arithmetic *is* a bit complex and difficult to grasp.

Then there are those who regard fishing as cruel. That is their prerogative. But if you want to see *really* 'cruel', just take a good look at life itself in the sea and you will see *seriously* cruel, or at least what *appears* to be cruel, for what occurs is not done with intent. For example on 30th April 2006, Australian TV's Channel 10 screened an article on their program 'I Fish' showing a couple of fishermen in a boat on a waterway where dolphins had just been on a feeding rampage amongst catfish. This was evidenced by numerous catfish heads floating by on the surface of the water. It was remarkable!

But that was just the beginning. One of the fishermen scooped up a number of these heads in his landing net where it could be seen that the dolphins had bitten off the bodies just behind the pectoral fins, thereby skilfully avoiding heads and fin spines. Even more incredibly, those heads were, without exception, still actively alive, breathing, and in many cases still attempting to move what was left of the body. Despite my long association with the sea and its ways, that scene was absolutely amazing to me – very revealing film footage.

The seas (like the lands) are killing fields. But they are, equally, living fields. Can one exist without the other?

Above: *I am still annoyed at not having caught whatever attacked the small fish at the bottom!*

Another example of how things work in the sea: the tailor (*Pomatomus saltatrix*) in the photograph above were caught in the surf north of the town of Rainbow Beach, Queensland, Australia, on an early June evening in 1998. The largest weighed 5 1/2 lbs. The smallest, at the bottom, was landed with a large part of its body missing; chopped off by an opportunistic relative as it was fighting on the end of my line! (The beer bottle to the left indicates the fishes' size, but has no other bearing on the story! It's a stubby, by the way, unfortunately not a 'long neck'!)

Some say cruelty is a matter of intent. Well, that's moving into philosophy, and this is not intended to be a book on philosophy – even if it does occasionally look that way. My next book will be, though. It's going to explain human nature. It will be a very, very long book. In the meantime I'll work on a 'live and let live basis'... well...except for fish that is.

Back to to a more serious note. After years of observation, reading and reflection, I have come to the conclusion that the instinctive programming of fish has just three facets – in no particular order:

1. Eat;
2. Avoid being eaten; and
3. Reproduce

This simple code has evolved into predatory, defensive and breeding behaviour so diverse, complex and successful that it almost defies belief. The seemingly limitless ingenuity of hunting, feeding, self-preservation and reproductive strategies of fish is, in the truest sense of the word, awesome!

Just as awesome for the angler, albeit in a slightly less scientific sort of way, is the fact that many of these behavioural patterns can be cleverly exploited to facilitate their capture. Now *that* is important!

On a slightly different matter: readers may already have noticed that pounds ('lb') rather than kilograms ('kg') are used in this book to give the weight of fish. The reason is obvious: it might be old fashioned but it looks bigger – why would anyone in their right mind use a system that makes their fish seem smaller? Naturally it is fine to express the weight of someone else's fish in kg; that is understandable. For those who insist on kg, divide lbs by 2.2 if you must.

For readers unfamiliar with the rigours of rock fishing, the line strength used may sometimes appear unsporting. I have often heard people speak as though there is a direct connection between line strength and fish weight – as though a thirty pound fish should be caught on line under thirty pounds in breaking strain, and that to catch one on heavier line is unsporting. In sandy, rock-free terrain, such as beach and some boat fishing, using lighter line is practicable, and in fact preferable as it will yield more strikes. In land-based rock fishing where equal or greater counter-force is often essential, aspects such as loss of line strength in knots, the ability of rocky and shellfish-encrusted terrain to sever taut nylon monofilament with ease, and the sheer pulling power of big fish in their initial run must be taken into account. Furthermore, the pulling power of a fishing rod – especially a long one – is usually only a fraction of the line's breaking strain and a large fish's strength.

These are debatable matters, but in rock fishing I believe it is better to land the fish quickly and, as far as is achievable, minimize the chance of a bust-up and fish escaping with tackle attached. A shorter fight is also more likely to yield higher survival prospects if fish are released.

On angling fish species, Australian rock anglers might be interested to learn of the South African 'steenbras' group of fish, as there is, for some strange reason, virtually no comparable species in Australian waters, the closest being the crab- and conjevoi-eating blue groper. These to me, are the 'big four' of rock fishing, but that excludes the pelagics which can also be formidable when hooked from the rocks.

The members of the steenbras group all grow large, and with the exception of the red steenbras which is nowadays rarely caught by land-based anglers, are reasonably easily accessible from the rocks – if you are prepared to put in the work. Photos of the latter three appear through the book. Their characteristics are as follows:

Red steenbras (*Petrus rupestris*).

Size: to over 110 lbs. Caught: mainly deep sea nowadays, but occasionally still from the rocks in deep water. Bait: Fresh fish fillet or whole fish, live-bait. Fight: extremely powerful and dirty fighter. Brief description: very good-looking fish. (No photos of this one unfortunately.)

Black steenbras, poenskop, blou biskop, stompkop (*Cymatoceps nasutus*).

Size: to 90 lbs. Caught: from rocks, usually in deeper water. Can be caught day or night. Bait: Live karanteen or shad (tailor), fresh fish fillet, head of a freshly caught shad (tailor), occasionally caught on rock crab, red bait (conjevoi), octopus or shellfish such as abalone. Occasionally on fresh pilchard. Fight: extremely powerful and dirty fighter. Brief description: bloody ugly fish...in a magnificent sort of a way.

Silver steenbras, musselcracker, beenbek (the latter meaning bone-jaw, *Sparodon durbanensis*).

Size: to at least 50 lbs. Caught: mainly from rocks, or where there is a mixture of rocks and sand. Daytime only. Bait: rock crab, conjevoi, abalone, and occasionally octopus. Fight: very powerful and dirty fighter. Brief description: strange, but definitely good looking.

White steenbras or pignose grunter (*Lithognathus lithognathus*).

Size: to at least 40 lbs. Caught: from predominantly sandy areas and in rivers. Mainly daytime, occasionally at night. Bait: sand or mud prawns, bigger specimens on rock crab. Occasionally on fresh pilchard. Fight: powerful but clean fighter. Brief description: really good-looking fish, almost in a feminine sort of way.

At last! That concludes the introductory topics. Time to move on to the juicy stuff. In Chapter 1, a few tales of hooks in the body are proffered as an early insight into the life of an angler (and those beings unfortunate enough to find themselves in his vicinity), and as a launching point for the rest of the book.

In Search Of Big Fish

Part One: South Africa

Chapter 1

The Early, Formative, but Mainly Fishless Years, Including a Few Hook-In-The-Body Stories

There is a point of disagreement in my family. Just the one of course, as we are an agreeable bunch, but it is an important one. Exactly when did my fishing career actually commence?

I say I was born with a fishing rod in my hand – a Conolon equipped with a Penn 49 'A' reel, loaded with 40 lb Atlas fishing line. My mother says no. So it comes down to opinion. I say mine was a direct experience (I was holding the fishing gear tightly at the time). My mother, on the other hand, is dependent upon casual observers and incidental bystanders who say there was no such thing. But such people are easily bribed and I stand by my version. I *know* I am right and that is all there is to it. Well, except perhaps to mention that my father, wishing to keep the peace, says that he himself was out fishing at the time and does not have an opinion.

The earliest fishing tales are a little empty of actual *catches* – but not of *incidents*. Two come immediately to mind. The first occurred when, at a guess, I was just eight or nine years old. My brother and I were fishing at a little blind estuary somewhere south of the South African coastal town of East London. This was a beautiful little town in

11

those days and it has at least two reasons to be proud – apart from its excellent fishing, that is. Firstly, it is named after some or other large city somewhere in Great Britain (I think) which also boasts a river port. Secondly, and, far more importantly, I was born there. Anyway we were fishing, and there were several spectators, amongst whom was a young lass of approximately my own age.

Now all through my fishing career there has been a shortage of female observers present at the right place, at the right time, to be impressed by my catches, or even by a demonstration of my skilful baiting techniques, casting prowess, or brilliant rock hopping talent ("Gee, isn't he *good* – sticks like a mountain goat – wonder if he'll talk to me") amongst many other possibilities. So, considering their rarity, this was an opportunity not to be wasted, and in an instant, I decided to use casting prowess as the demonstration of choice.

I swung to cast, sending hook and sinker whistling out in a wide, sweeping arc, streaking through the air, rod bending in a beautiful curve as the forces of speed and resistance increased exponentially. (Well…that's how it all felt anyway.) I was in my element.

Then to my amazement: WAPPP-WHOA!!! Solid resistance behind me where resistance should *not* have happened. I spun around to the sound of the little girl's sudden piercing screams, and my rapture ended abruptly and horribly. They were not screams of admiration. My hook and (fortunately very small) sinker were swinging from her ear, her hands were raised next to her head, and she was shaking in horror, pain and disbelief.

CATCHING A "VENUS EAR"

I don't remember in any detail the events which followed, which included my parents' apologies along with my own – for I was certainly remorseful – and the little girl's departure for the nearest doctor. We stopped fishing and went home after that.

Some time later when the dust had settled slightly, I proudly referred to the incident as my capture of a 'Venus Ear' (which is a common name for abalone or *'perlemoen'* shellfish in South Africa). The inevitable adult presence at the time was not amused. (There was *always* an adult presence in those days, unlike approval, which was rare. Maybe that had something to do with me?)

There was another incident in my early fishing career involving a fish hook finding its way into a person rather than a fish. This time the person was me.

I became an enthusiastic fisherman at a very young age. If I couldn't actually be fishing then the next best thing was to indulge in an associated activity such as casting practice. And so it came to pass that at age eight or thereabouts (that age *again* – it was a bad era!), I was practising casting while holidaying with my parents at the police camp at Port Edward on the Natal South Coast of South Africa. A new 'coffee grinder' reel was the focus of my activities. This type of reel is called an 'egg beater' in Australia – both delightful and quite accurately descriptive names for these quaint but effective contraptions.

Like many who endeavour to master the idiosyncrasies of these reels, I was having more than a little difficulty in timing the sinker's release. This meant that the sinker would either hit the ground a pace or two in front of me, its considerable force producing a thud and puff of dust, or it would take off vertically and disappear into space while I waited fearfully below, hands over my head, eyes screwed up in anticipation. In this case too, it would return to mother earth with a thud and puff of dust – unless it landed on my head in which case the thud would be duller and there might be a puff of dandruff instead of dust, and an exclamation of pain.

Ah yes, and just very occasionally it would take off at the desired angle, or in the desired direction. (Though even then never both at the same time.) On the occasion of the practice session in question there were no witnesses – wisdom or fear had long since ensured their departure to safer territory, potentially avoiding a costly lawsuit against my family.

On this cast, the last in that particular session, the sinker took off over a low overhead telephone wire and plopped down on the other side, leaving me with a predicament – how to retrieve it? I immediately decided with impulsive good cheer and ingenuity to simply throw the sinker back over the telephone wire and continue my practising. This probably would have worked had there not, for the sake of authenticity, been a small hook included on the rig.

I threw the sinker and dangling hook with all the force I could muster… "WAPPP-WHOA!!!" And "EEYEEEEOOWW!!!" This time the yell was my own. The hook was embedded in my finger. *Deep* in my finger. My predicament had increased multi-fold and now included pain, helplessness *and* embarrassment. I was also suddenly part of the telecommunication system. Not that my yells needed any wiry assistance to carry *them* through the ether. My parents, immediately recognizing their offspring's personal brand of sound – thanks to frequent exposure rather than any miracle of nature – came hastily to my rescue, heaving heavy sighs of resignation, eyes pointing skyward. (Perhaps they thought there could still be more bits of fishing tackle raining down.)

And, as in the case of my young female victim in the previous incident, I too was whisked off to the nearest doctor ("My, my, what have we here?") and my first exposure to the joys of local anaesthesia.

EEYEEEOOWW!

Later in my fishing career I was to experience more such interactions with fish hooks, one of them substantial, as the photograph in a later chapter reveals. Why do I have a photograph of it? Who knows – maybe I had a premonition I was going to write a book and *knew* people would love to see a picture of a large fish hook in my hand. Or maybe the photographer – a wonderful fishing companion of many marvellous and eventful trips, and a talented photographer - had a strange taste in topics pictorial.

Actually, upon reflecting on my 'close association' with hooked fishing equipment over the years, I can only conclude that the attraction is genetic. There is yet *another* event which could easily have put an early end to my fishing career – or any other kind of career for that matter – by almost putting an end to *me*.

My father had taken me with him on an early morning fishing excursion to the East London harbour breakwater, or 'the breakwall' as it was known. This was a rare and treasured event as the wall was the fishermen's 'rough end of town' and really no place for a kid of my young age. In good weather, hardened fishermen would cover it, and in bad weather huge waves would do likewise. And large fish seemed to frequent it in all weather. To get a better view of the angling activities, while my father fished I climbed up onto the base of the flashing beacon situated at the end of the breakwall. To steady myself, I clung to the sign which said 'ABSOLUTELY NO UNAUTHORISED PERSONS ALLOWED' or words to that effect.

The breakwall was an excellent, productive fishing venue and before long the cry "GAFF, **GAFF, *GAAAFFF!!!*"** rent the air over the slop and splash of the sea against its huge interlocking concrete blocks or 'dolosse' as they were called. Someone had hooked into a big fish and he wanted a gaff at the ready – *NOW!* Within seconds there was the splish/splash of a man running hastily along the slippery wet concrete, a long gaff waving about as he used it to balance himself. As he rushed past me, my genetic hook-attraction engaged and the gaff hook found itself unable to whistle safely past. Instead – WHACK! – the hook smacked solidly into the back of my head.

Miraculously, it immediately bounced back out and the runner didn't even look round, probably thinking – if he noticed it at all – that the gaff hook had struck and bounced off the beacon itself.

My head bled profusely, but how the gaff hook didn't rip my scalp wide open or throw me metres down onto the concrete below – or into the sea beyond that – is a mystery. Maybe survival is also in my genes. This was just the first of several close encounters of the bloody scary kind in the course of my fishing career. (The fish for which the gaff was intended, by the way, was a large kob, or Australian mulloway/jewfish, *Argyrosomus hololepidotus*.)

The next story, although getting at least a little closer to some actual fish-catching action, is to me, a very sad one.

The venue was once again the East London harbour breakwall. My father and I were there by first signs of light, right at the end of the wall. He was throwing a home-made solid tin 'spoon' (lure) with a substantial 'S' curve bent into it to produce a vigorous movement at slow speed. The pure tin could easily be manipulated by hand, producing a characteristic creaking sound as it bent. (See photograph later on in the book.) On this occasion the spoon was being retrieved slowly over the sandy bottom in the hope of attracting a kob.

Before long – SMACK! – he hooked into a good fish. Being rather a gentleman and definitely not the standard 'wall fisherman' kind of bloke, my father did not wish to interrupt anyone else's fishing too early in the action, so he waited a while before calling for a gaff. Eventually the fish started to tire and was persuaded to approach the surface. The end was theoretically in sight. Time to call for a gaff, and he did so with the same fervour as recounted earlier. "GAFF....... **GAFF.........** *GAAAFFFFF!!!......... CAN SOMEONE PLEASE BRING A GAFF?"*

But alas, my father was not one of the 'boys' – not one of the fraternity who frequented the wall in the quest for recognition in the fishing column of the local newspaper, the Daily Dispatch – and so his calls went unheeded. The 'boys' were about helping their own, not an outsider with his young kid – neither of whom, they would have felt, belonged there anyway. My father's shouts continued in vain until the kob of around 40 lbs eventually found its way into the blocks and cut itself free. A little later as we left the wall to go home we noticed a long gaff close by, partially hidden in the concrete blocks. I felt devastated and incredulous. I can only imagine how my father felt and I do not recall him ever going to the wall again, with or without me.

As a result of this disgustingly unsporting event, I subsequently made it my business *always* to retrieve my line and ready my own gaff instantly when *any* fellow angler hooked a decent fish. I have gaffed many large fish for other fishermen and do not recall ever losing anyone else's fish at the gaff, though I have lost an uncomfortable number of my own while fishing alone and attempting to gaff them myself – a practice I do *not* advocate for others.

My youthful fishing career, which, although it sowed a seed of 'giant beanstalk' proportions in terms of desire to fish, admittedly consisted somewhat more of observation than participation, though I do recall catching my first fish – a 'bully' out of a rock pool, followed by a large blacktail and a rock cod. This all came to a tragic end at age thirteen when my family moved from East London to Johannesburg. As hard as I tried, fishing for carp or stunted tilapia in the stagnant waters of the mine dams of Benoni or Boksburg in the shadow of mine dumps, or in the dam at the Modderfontein Dynamite factory under weeping willow trees, just didn't 'cut it' for me. Neither did fishing in the Vaal river (on any day of the week except Sunday in the 'Free State' unless you wanted to earn God's wrath and a fine), even though, compared with the dams, it was almost paradise with its actually 'moving' water. Mind you, you had to look quite carefully to see the movement and there couldn't be a drought on…

No, Johannesburg and surrounds didn't do much for me, though it worked for those who would regard themselves as fishing when snoozing in a folding chair, beer in hand, hoping the 'mieliepap policeman' wouldn't bob up and down and disturb them too frequently.

For the benefit of those unacquainted with a fisherman's mieliepap policeman, mieliepap bait is made from steamed maize meal, prepared so as to produce a stiff, stodgy consistency that can be moulded into a lump of bait on a fish hook. Some species of fish, such as carp, which must be desperately hungry, will actually eat this. A mieliepap policeman is the admittedly quite ingenious South African device used by the folding-chair-fishing-brigade to alert them to a kurper (tilapia), barbel or carp tapping tentatively at their earthworm or custard/curry flavoured mieliepap bait. After the bait has been cast into the turbid depths and the fishing rod balanced on a rod holder pushed into the muddy river bank or dam edge, a small piece of the same mieliepap bait is squished into a tight little ball over the fishing line. With careful observation, this rather cleverly named 'policeman' can be seen to twitch as an aquatic denizen attacks the bait in a typical freshwater-fish feeding frenzy.

But I dreamed of REAL fish, of the 'hit a big live-bait' and 'smoking run' kind.

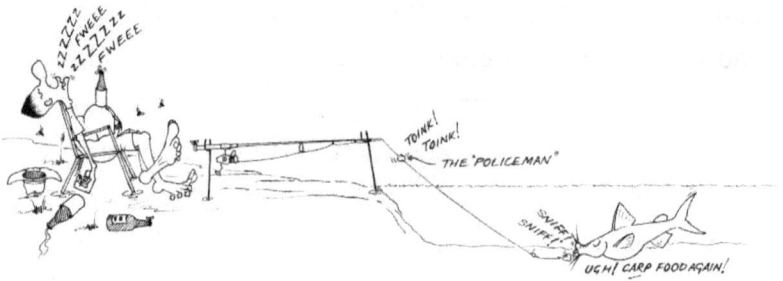

A barbel feeding frenzy

I couldn't wait to swap the almost imperceptible bob of a mieliepap policeman for the roar of oceanic swells smashing on vertical cliffs – the voice of an ocean saying, "I guard these beauties in my depths, come and get them if you dare."

Chapter 2

Back To The Sea! The Move to the West Coast of South Africa, With Some Funny Events, But Still Few Fish

I managed to return to the sea after leaving high school in Johannesburg, thank God – even if, initially, it turned out to be not quite what I had hoped…

After leaving school and completing my (then) compulsory military training, I set about finding employment. Several fish-associated businesses were approached in the hope of finding some sort of fish-related employment. (I was 'fish crazy', not just about angling, but about anything to do with fish.) Two producers of frozen fish responded. Irvin and Johnson in Cape Town said no.

Sea Harvest in Saldanha said yes. *Frozen* fish! Fortunately I wasn't fussy – I was off to the sea again. I ached with joy.

This joy was immeasurably heightened by the fact that accompanying me was a Suzuki 250 cc motorcycle, packed into a large wooden crate. The fact that it was ancient – either the first production motorcycle Suzuki ever built, or an experimental prototype – was immaterial. I wasn't just elated, I was euphoric! The bike featured in many a fishing trip. Alas, Saldanha was not a fishing venue in which the Suzuki became overloaded with fish, but it was certainly a big part of the adventure for a young school leaver. At this stage my fishing career consisted of little experiences inspiring big dreams which fed enormous ambitions.

Saldanha, although contributing usefully to my learning curve, *still* did not yield big edible fish (this is made up for later in the book), but it did have its fascinations and unique flavour, and served to further whet an already huge appetite for fishing.

One of Saldanha's best known piscatorial features is the Cape snoek (*Thyrsites atun*), present at times in great numbers, reasonably close to shore. This slender, black, oily (and toothy) fish makes superb eating when smoked, but is very bony and sometimes full of parasitic worms in the flesh, which, believe it or not, are considered to be a good thing by some – *not* including myself. Nevertheless, I did occasionally get to eat infested specimens and lived to fish another day. This amazing fish didn't feature so much in my angling records as in my medical records...

On several occasions I was invited by two elderly acquaintances – one of them a Mr Roland Turvey, the late father of 'Topsy Turvey' the well known South African aerobatics pilot – to join them on deep sea 'snoeking' expeditions. I am not quite sure if the invitations came my way because I was 'such a pleasant young man to have along' or because their boat's diesel engine was such a bastard to crank. Either way I joined them, cranked the engine, and fished for snoek in the usual way, using a 'dollie' – a cylindrical piece of lead about ten centimetres long with a thin hole through it. Through this hole, one end of a fairly short but very heavy nylon hand-line was passed and attached to a *very* large hook, such that the hook was positioned below the dollie, with its eye up against it.

This was thrown over the gunwale, allowed to sink a few metres, then 'worked' by jerking it up and down or pulling it rapidly upwards through the water. If the snoek were feeding, the dollie would be attacked within seconds, and a short but vigorous fight would ensue until the fish was brought on board. Once on deck the critter would *really* begin to fight. Unless one had mastered the rapid 'under-arm-neck-break-manoeuvre,' any human body part in the area was in grave danger from fish fangs and the dollie hook. The slippery fish would slash and flap around and be very difficult to grab and hold onto.

This was bad enough, but there was a far more insidious danger – bad enough for me to believe it was yet another of Neptune's cunning devices to discourage fishermen. The snoek's sharp and spiky body parts, *especially* the teeth, are home to very virile bacteria, and even the smallest cut or scratch – virtually unavoidable under the circumstances – would be 'open season' to them. I became acquainted with them after my first or second trip, and they struck again on several subsequent occasions. What made them particularly nasty is that they would only manifest in the human body a few days after the fishing event itself was over – exactly coinciding with the time when stories of conquest and victory had reached the pinnacle of permissible exaggeration:

"We really got into the snoek this time – taught 'em a lesson – showed 'em who's boss. How many? Aw, too many to keep track of, y'know. Bloody big too – didn't measure 'em but the biggest I've seen for years. Didn't see any other boats with such big ones, mind you."

In a fashion rather reminiscent of Pinocchio's nose, such boasts obviously spurred the bacteria into action. By breakfast next morning the area surrounding a tiny, hardly visible scratch on one of my hands would have reddened and become a little hot, swollen and tender. By morning tea time a red streak would have started its clearly visible journey up my arm to a gland in my armpit and I'd be *SORE*. By lunch time, hand throbbing, armpit aching and head spinning, I would be in the doctor's waiting room wishing he'd hurry his bloody self up! I would be in very considerable discomfit and certain I was going to die.

The local medical fraternity was well acquainted (albeit it probably not by direct experience) with the offending organisms' destructive capacity and speed of infection, and the antibiotic cure came in a syringe rather than in the more user-friendly capsule form. By that stage I didn't 'givashit'. I knew by word of mouth and observation that many of the local fishing population sported a shortened (or totally missing) finger or two, and felt that even if I didn't die I was at least destined to lose a limb.

"Please stick the bloody needle in and get it over with! Ouch ...FFFU...Thank you."

I always tried to be polite to the doctors – one never knew when one might need their services again under similar or other critical circumstances. The cure was remarkably rapid. Bodily normality returned first, followed immediately by bravado – the latter clearly indicating a full recovery.

"It was nothing really. Are we going out Saturday – the boys are catching heaps... We'll show 'em who's boss...!"

P.S. With its severe mouth-bacteria problem, the snoek must rank very high on the list of sea-dwelling halitosis sufferers. Or rather, presumably, as in the case of humans, the so-called 'sufferer' doesn't suffer at all...but those in the immediate vicinity...!!!

EEYUKK!
THE BREATH!
SOD OFF
SYDNEY!

HHHELLO SNOEKUMS
HHH OW ABOUT IT?

Saldanha is situated on the south west coast of South Africa. The water is relatively cold and nutrient-rich. Typically, this should be home to large numbers of a few species rather than smaller numbers of many species, as is more characteristic of warmer waters.

Well, that's the theory. But after fishing in these waters with great youthful passion and vigour, I developed another hypothesis. My efforts revealed a fact of great biological significance – to Saldanha anglers, that is. It is abundantly evident that the higher fish species-diversity of the warmer waters to the east, and the great fish numbers in the cooler waters to the north *each disappear before actually reaching Saldanha itself,* leaving a sort of 'no man's land' or rather, 'no fishes' water' kind of situation in the immediate area. A near fishless void in my opinion.

Commercial catches in the area would greatly contradict this but I was line fishing from the rocks and beaches, not using a trawler. Even the famed snoek which were said to 'come in quite close' and the giant pignose grunter (*Lithognathus lithognathus*) which was said to frequent Langebaan Lagoon at certain times of the year, eluded me, though I do remember catching a lot of too-small-to-keep 'piggies' at a river mouth a few kilometres to the north.

What *were* present in large numbers were sharks and rays of various kinds, but my interest lay in 'edible' fish and they were scarce. Even the west coast Hottentot fish (*Pachymetopon blochii*) though present in large numbers around the local islands, were neither plentiful nor particularly large in the areas accessible to the purely land-based angler.

So as I said, my motorbike, though making many trips with fishing rods tied to its crash bars, was never excessively burdened by the weight of fresh fish. Sea air and salt spray eventually took their toll and brought its usefulness to an end. The last trip I remember making with it was to a fishing spot called Paternoster, on a rainy Christmas day in the early nineteen seventies. Caring friends tried to discourage me.

"Would you like to join us for Christmas dinner?"

"No thank you, I'm going fishing!"

"But it's pouring cats and bloody dogs!"

"I can see that, thanks anyway – bye now."

And off I went on the Suzuki. By this stage of its rather hard life it had started to shock me through the handle bars in wet or even damp weather. This was unpredictable and extremely unpleasant, not to mention dangerous – even at the bike's modest maximum speed. Technically, how this could actually occur was a mystery to me, but it certainly did. Not being mechanically minded myself, and not having the funds to pay someone else to fix the problem, it stayed unfixed and worsened progressively. I remember it being terrible on that wet Christmas day, and shortly thereafter I decided I'd had enough and got rid of it. Whether someone subsequently looked at it for two seconds, snipped off an offending electric wire and got zillions more shock-free kilometres out of it, I neither know nor care.

The Suzuki was replaced by a 1960 model, 500 cc ex-police BMW motorbike, a beautiful machine that served dependably for many years, rods and gaff tied to its crash bars, fishing gear in its single fibreglass pannier. (While I owned the bike I seemed never quite able to afford a second pannier. Fishing tackle took precedence.) This bike was greatly instrumental in finally launching me into some really *good* fishing – *at last!*

As a result of Saldanha's poor fishing, when rare opportunity permitted I used to travel, rods 'n all, across the Cape Province through the Karoo to the delightfully scenic town of Knysna on the south east Cape coast, a fishing paradise by comparison. On one such trip, some friends told me of a job for a bacteriologist being advertised at Table Top Foods (frozen vegetables) in the town of

George – they knew I would LOVE to move to the area. I protested.

"I know nothing of bacteriology!"

"They will teach you," they encouraged patiently.

"I'm on a motorbike with fishing rods and gaff tied to it, for Pete's sake!"

"They won't care," they said, still patiently.

"But I only have these tatty fishing clothes and ancient, bait-impregnated old leather jacket!"

"They will be interested in *you*, not your clothes! Now *get* on the phone and *phone* them for an interview," they pressed, losing patience with my protests.

"OK, *OK…*!" I knew when I was beaten and got on the phone and made an appointment. As predicted they didn't care about the peripherals and I got the job.

(Just before this event, my existing employer in Saldanha, Sea Harvest, had offered me the opportunity to do a year-long diploma course in food technology, at company expense, salary included. *Food technology!* Who the hell wants to study *food technology* when there's fishing to be done???)

Chapter 3

The Eastern Cape Coast: Catching Crabs For Bait, Drinking Sea Water, A Terrible Smell, An Angling Wager, And My First Musselcracker!

And so I moved to wonderland, brimming – nay, overflowing – with youthful excitement and anticipation. I doubt whether it could have been more than mere hours after arriving in the town of George and finding a place to sleep and house my belongings before I was off in search of what was on offer fishing-wise.

Over a period of several years the area did not disappoint in number, size or variety. However, the musselcracker (*Sparodon durbanensis*) proved to be the indisputable king as they were not only big and powerful, but quite readily available if you were prepared to put in the work.

This magnificent coastline, especially the Mossel Bay, George, Knysna and Plettenburg Bay stretch, was famous for its 'musselcracker runs' starting in late October, peaking in November, and fading in December. I knew of this famous fish and wanted one *badly*, having never landed one thus far. Some time in late October of 1973, a friend challenged me to a bet of a six-pack of beers for whoever caught the first 'cracker of the season. He was on! It would not only be my first 'cracker of the season, it would be my first 'cracker *ever*! I didn't need beer to spur me on, but then again, it certainly wouldn't hinder my efforts.

One of the finest baits for musselcracker is the red rock crab *Plagusia chabrus*. Musselcracker know them well (though presumably not by that name) and love them. They will effortlessly take a crab of 150 mm leg span or more. Although best used alive or very fresh, they easily shed their legs while being put on the hook, and keeping all the legs attached can be difficult when working with them alive. They *can* be tied onto the hook whilst still alive using cotton or a rubber band or two, but it is easier to freeze them and use freshly defrosted ones. There is also the concern that if still alive they might be able to crawl into a rocky hole and hide from the fish – a most unacceptable eventuality!

Catching them during the day or at high tide is difficult to say the least – they are very wide awake and quick-moving though they can sometimes be located by feeling under seaweedy rock ledges. The problem is that these are sometimes also home to other creatures with a disposition even less welcoming to human hands than crabs – which are none too friendly themselves when disturbed in this way.

Rock crabs are most easily caught at night in rock pools at low tide. At night, for some inexplicable reason, although they are very much exposed, out and about doing whatever crabs do, they are remarkably easily approached. But do not be lulled here into a false sense of 'this is a cinch' by their apparent somnambulatory appearance. It is possible to pin them to the rock surface by firm pressure with a finger or two on the carapace (back of the body) which renders them relatively helpless because the nippers are then restricted in their movement. (The *actual extent* of this restriction is rapidly learned by experience.) Similarly, they can be lifted by gripping the body (approached from *behind*) with two fingers on top of the body and the thumb below, while still maintaining adequate pressure on the body with the first hand. Or this can be done with the thumb on the front between the eyes, two fingers gripping the back. Again, in these positions their range of attack is restricted. And again, experience is the quickest teacher of the *range* of this restriction. It may be helpful here to mention that there is precious little margin of safety either way.

Once lifted, if not before, they wake up and immediately react with considerable indignation – which, right at the top of the list, includes powerful nipping. It now becomes a tussle between 'I want bait' and 'I want freedom' and only the most determined bait-seeker will be able to hang on or hang in. Sometimes it is the crab that gets to do the hanging on, but believe me, this is not because it is offering its services as bait – no sirrree. Fingers are understandably targeted, and they hold on tenaciously. Many times, with a gasp and popping eyes, I have literally had to lift a crab to my mouth and bite the offending nipper in two to break its grip. This was done *very* carefully, all the while ensuring that the second nipper was firmly held and not allowed to find facial purchase – which it *would* have done, given half a chance. Of course the crab *could* be flicked away when it first attached to the finger, which would solve the problem, but this would also mean losing the crab – *unthinkable!*

The next requirement is to get them into a bucket with a lid where, unfortunately, they seem to think that their captured brethren are part of the problem, and appendages may be lost.

Some seaweed helps. The crabs are then taken home and frozen, after which the sooner they are used, the better. I made countless such middle-of-the-night crab-collecting trips, though always taking only what could be used within the next few days.

NOTE that the laws for different areas pertaining to the collection of all baits need to be ascertained and adhered to – if not for the obviously essential reason of conserving stocks, then, for those who don't think that extensively, because the pain of a heavy fine or confiscation of equipment can make the nip of even a large crab pale into insignificance. (Not to mention the embarrassment!)

On a slightly different subject for a moment, on one interesting occasion I was, surprisingly, able to capture three or four bait crabs during the day at a spot near Ballot's Bay north of Victoria Bay, the latter being a well known Cape surfing venue. I had arrived very early in the morning and had worn a large, heavy, waterproof coat against the chill. I had no suitable container for the crabs so I placed them in one of the large coat pockets for temporary safekeeping.

After a deceptively chilly start, the day put its temperature setting onto 'HOT' and left it there. It got hotter and hotter as the hours wore on. By noon it was *extremely* hot and as usual I had brought no drinking water with me. (It took me innumerable *desperately* thirsty fishing trips before I learned to carry water – *and* to take warm gear if I was going out at night. I got to saying, "I won't be thirsty, it won't be cold tonight 'cos it's warm now," and paying the price one time too many. Thank God my actual angling learning-curve wasn't that slow!)

Anyway, this was just such a desperately thirsty occasion – I was probably developing gall stones on the spot. But I was alone and miles from drinking-water. I was fishing and wasn't going anywhere. (Fishermen can be *very* stubborn.) The tide was in and the sea water was crystal clear and splashing tantalisingly about the rock pools. It danced and frothed and bubbled, and looked cool and refreshing in the oppressive heat. And eventually, yes, it began to make me think of lemonade. It looked just like it, and by then my thirst was veritably screaming at me. I wasn't anywhere near to actually losing my marbles (I like to think) but eventually I became convinced that anything that looked so good simply couldn't taste so bad. This conclusion was arrived at despite the fact that I had on many occasions had unwanted mouthfuls of sea water when skin diving and swimming in the surf – and *knew* how foul the stuff tastes! Finally thirst overpowered logic, memory and all other solid dependable things, and I bent over a sparkling pool. I didn't just scoop the water up delicately in my hands; I stuck my face in it and sucked like a horse.

EEEOOORRGGGHHH!!!! Mistake! *BIG* mistake! Anyone who has ever drunk – or even sipped – sea water, for whatever reason, will know that the instant it touches the oesophagus the body will vigorously activate its most potent repulse mechanism. More violently so if it is gulped and swallowed. Well anyway, that's what mine did. My stomach heaved so convulsively to repel the vile intruder that I thought it was going to rupture my innards. I have never repeated the exercise. Dying of thirst seems preferable.

There were in any case no fish around. They would have been sheltering in the shade somewhere, drinking that beautiful cool water – *they* wouldn't have cared about its saltiness. I decided to pack it in.

I went home, put away my gear and hung my coat in the wardrobe. I was a bachelor, at the time boarding in a communal household. There was no such luxury as a garage or storeroom for storing fishing gear. Everything lived in my bedroom except the rods. They were housed on the veranda. My bedroom was well known for its varying degrees of fishing-related odours. *I* thought they were at best quite pleasant, on average no problem, and at worst quite acceptable. Co-residents disagreed and I had long since been relegated to the bedroom situated furthest from everyone else's. This suited me well as I could also come and go at odd hours of the night on fishing trips without disturbing anyone. A supply of fresh fish (I haven't got to that bit yet but it did eventually happen) just tipped the scales of content/discontent in my favour and thus it was that a delicate peace reigned over the household.

That was, until a new and somehow slightly different odour began to emanate insidiously from somewhere in my bedroom. Even I noticed it and was a little taken aback. The puzzlement response lasted a day or two as the smell worsened. I was used to smells. A damp fishing bag encrusted with dried bait of varying kinds and soaked with similarly sourced fluids was the usual culprit and a good wash and airing would normally fix this. On this occasion I wouldn't have been concerned except out of consideration for the house's other occupants, but the smell worsened and my thoughts even turned to my own well-being as they began to make ugly threats. The infamous fishing bag had long since been given a comprehensive sniff-over. Despite being a little niffy, it was innocent of any major offence – but something wasn't. You could almost see the pong.

By my reckoning, if that smell had been visible, it would have been a dense mauve/purple colour with yellow blotches. It was a nauseating, sour, advanced rottingliquifying flesh sort of a smell, even worse than when a dog rolls in something disgusting. At the time I just couldn't fathom it. It was inexplicable.

That I eventually homed in on the source was thanks to maggots – which I don't normally thank for their presence anywhere. These eventually led me to my large coat in the wardrobe, and ultimately to the pocket containing the now dissolving crabs which I had placed there many days before – for their temporary safe-keeping – and promptly forgotten about. Their natural decomposition had been enthusiastically assisted by dozens of writhing maggots which themselves had quite understandably finally become so offended by the overpowering rank, putrid smell that they had decided to vacate. I almost felt sorry for them. (How their parents found their way into the wardrobe in the first place remains a mystery, but they did.)

Opening the pocket to remove the contents and wash the inside was not pleasant and took many repeat performances with hot water and concentrated cleaning agents. The event was long remembered in the household and referred to at my expense, but it blew over at last and a fragile peace and acceptance reigned once again, sustained by the occasional fresh fish.

Left: *One of the fresh fish used as a peacemaker in the communal household. Note the old leather jacket of interview fame, that smelled of herbs from sleeping on a 'shrubby bush' bed at the famous fishing venue of Robberg. (It also smelled of old bait.)*

Now, where was I before I got onto the subject of crabs? Ah yes, the first musselcracker. One afternoon I parked my BMW motorbike at the end of a dirt track leading through the bushes to a fishing spot near the town of George called 'Die Kerel' meaning 'the fellow' or 'chap'. I am not sure why it was so named. 'Bloody Hard Walk' would have been more fitting. For that matter, to simplify things I could have called most of my favourite spots 'bloody hard walk' and just numbered them. I goated my way down the steep, loose-surfaced stony path, fighting my fishing rods and gaff through the surrounding tough, scrubby coastal bushes. Sweating and puffing I arrived on the rocks.

The afternoon was beautiful – windless, warm and sunny. By preference I usually fish for musselcracker in the very early morning, but they will occasionally take a bait through the day. The sea was magnificent though a little on the calm side for 'cracker, which tend to feed more freely in turbulent white water. I had that familiar feeling of elation and gratitude that I was 'there again'. I never took my much loved fishing trips for granted. As I unpacked my gear, the blood in my veins was replaced by a river of anticipation and excitement. Heaven *is* on earth, and I was there.

I went through the motions of rigging up with a heavy sinker and 9/0 or 10/0 hook on 45 lb line. (I soon upgraded to 50 and ultimately 60 lb line for targeting musselcracker and poensies when I realized how powerful their first run could be, though I still landed some while fishing with lighter tackle.) 'Cracker are hard, dirty fighters which make for the rocks at every opportunity. Their large shellfish-crushing teeth and jaws will engulf a large rock crab without hesitation and crush it to pulp in seconds. No sense in using light tackle to subdue these rock dwelling power-houses.

I made up two rods, both heavy poles with tightly secured Penn 49 'A' reels. A defrosted crab was affixed to the hook on one outfit. I wet the line on the reel from a small rock pool, and was ready to cast. (Failing to wet the line first was likely to produce severe burns on the thumb that controlled the flow of line as it screamed off the reel during the cast. Such omissions could not only leave a very painful white burn on the thumb, but also damage even heavy nylon – which would then leave unpleasant doubts in the angler's mind...)

I had already surveyed the area while I was making up the rods. I was standing on the moderately rough red/orange rocks which sloped reasonably gently down to the sea. I had fished the area before, but not this exact spot. The terrain in front of me was quite 'tame', that is, calm and not particularly rugged-appearing in terms of its rocky bottom. This was as far as I could estimate through the quite clear and relatively shallow water and the exposed rocks in the vicinity. I had already located a place in the rocks where I could land a good fish – a critical prerequisite for any fishing spot where large fish are targeted. Many potentially excellent spots cannot be fished because it would simply be too difficult or dangerous (or impossible) to land a decent fish. To add to the problem in my case, I fished alone most of the time.

I chose a promising looking area of sea. This was the only patch of turbulent choppy water in the area, into which blue water plunged and boiled each time a swell heaved over a nearby rocky outcrop. Having established a steady footing on the rocks I hurled the heavy rig as hard as I could, successfully placing the bait exactly where I wanted it. Acceptable accuracy and distance were by no means always achieved on the first throw, and because I was painfully particular about where I placed the bait, this often meant retrieving the rig, replacing the crab if it was damaged (I was *very* particular about that too), and casting out again.

At first I stood at the ready, holding the rod, full of initial optimism in anticipation of an early pick-up (bite). After ten or fifteen minutes of waiting, poised for action, my optimism turned to realism. It was rare to get a pick-up on a slow bait such as a crab so quickly, especially in the mid-afternoon, though it could happen. I then went into my usual routine: finding as accommodating a rock formation as possible, sitting down, and waiting for my posterior to adjust itself to the contours of the chosen rocks. (I feel it is my duty to give some advice here. It is said that sitting on cold, damp rocks for prolonged periods can cause severe haemorrhoids. Unhappily, I can confirm this.)

This position was, after a few butt-adjusting movements, far more comfortable than standing, and I settled in for a long wait. Crab baits have the very great advantage of being relatively immune to the onslaught of 'peckers' – small fish that can either strip a good bait down to nothing or render it unacceptable to larger fish. I have had crabs taken by big fish after a wait of as long as two hours, though it is wise to check their condition far sooner than that – it's not good to sit with an empty hook for too long; fishing time is precious!

On this occasion an hour might have passed without a hint of action before I decided to wedge the first rod securely in a crack in the rocks, and bait up the second so that I could have two lines out. I often fished in this way when things were quiet and easier prey was being sought.

However although one's chances are doubled, I did not normally do so when using crab for bait, as the target was musselcracker and they were hard enough to hook even when holding the rod. To add to this, they often bit very slyly in calm conditions and great skill was needed to hook them. But things were so quiet I decided to relax a little and ten minutes later both baits were out and both rods were wedged securely in the rocks.

It was a warm, lazy sort of a day. With a rod on either side of me, the reels' ratchets engaged, drags set hard enough to hook a fish but not to break the line (or rods), and a hand on each to bring any enquiry rapidly to my attention, I leaned backwards and relaxed totally. Despite my rocky seat, in the relaxing warmth my thoughts turned to daydreams, and daydreams turned to real dreams. It was blissful to say the least.

However, this was a business trip, and before drifting off into that peaceful state, I knew that I didn't *really* want the peaceful state to last. And it didn't. Some time after unconsciousness had overwhelmed me, one of the rods jerked forward and its reel screamed. To be wrenched from deep unconsciousness to full consciousness so abruptly and violently must surely pose a serious risk to one's heart – at least for the fraction of a second before adrenalin comes to the rescue, fixes the heart and gets the mind functioning properly again.

Against the odds, the fish had hooked itself solidly without any assistance from me. But there was an immediate problem. The fish's powerful, sustained pull against a fairly tight drag kept the rod firmly stuck in its rocky crevice despite my vigorous efforts to free it. Frantically I hauled against the fish's run to neutralise the wedging force. At last, amply adrenalin-assisted, I managed to free the rod and just as I fumbled to disengage the still screaming ratchet, the run stopped and I was able to re-gather my composure. But there was no time to relax. The discontinued run meant the fish had either reached a refuge or was looking for one. And refuge to a musselcracker means rocks – rocks that are home to myriad sharp things that cut through even heavy nylon line with ease. I fought to turn the tables – the tables in this case being the fish's big head.

The battle plan exercised by most musselcrackers is a relatively short but enormously powerful run, which, unless one has very strong equipment or is *very* lucky, usually terminates with the fish cutting itself free amongst the rocks. My effort was focussed on turning its head at all costs. This could well break the line, but failure to stop the fish was likely to be just as costly. On this occasion I succeeded in turning the fish and ending that high risk period, tipping the battle in my favour – at least for the moment. The fish's counter-plunges and head-jerks continued. This resulted in a little line being taken occasionally in short dashes, but relentless 'lift and wind' pressure on my part ensured that the fish remained shore-bound. Eventually, now rapidly tiring, the fish allowed me to guide its movement it until the landing site was reached. As the distance between the fish and myself decreased, I progressively lightened the drag so that any last minute dash or pull of backwash would not result in a broken line – an eventuality that still managed to occur in later years when I made a bad decision while I was playing an enormous fish on the Transkei coast. (The horrors of this are recounted in detail later – a very bad memory to this day!)

Above: *The first musselcracker! Weighing 15 lb, it was taken on crab in 1973 near George in the Cape.*

"MY FIRST *MUSSELCRACKER*!!! YAH – BLOODY – *HOO!!!*"

With the fisherman-friendly sea running at this time, I was able to choose a light swell to lift the now barely struggling fish up the rocks to within reach. Then holding it hard in that position as the water turned and rushed back down around and over it, I waited anxiously until I could reach under the bottom of a gill with my right hand and lift and carry it, with only a shake or two, to the safety of higher rocks and a deep pool. This achieved, relief and elation struck simultaneously.

Apart from the very fortunate chance-hooking of the fish, which was especially surprising in the calm conditions, the course of events was fairly typical – a very powerful first run, some strong attempts at a dash for cover, but thanks to adequately heavy tackle, a short and diminishing struggle after that. With lighter tackle the fight would have been more prolonged and challenging but had a far greater chance of a negative outcome.

The story doesn't quite end there. Hoping, as fisherman do, for a little more action, I launched a new crab out to sea, having pulled in the second line and found the bait missing, presumably crushed with impunity in a luckier musselcracker's maw. I was also fully aware of how extremely fortunate I had been that the fighting fish had not got tangled in this second line – a strong drawback to fishing alone with two lines out.

I waited patiently without further action until the sun dipped behind the hill – which I still had to climb – bringing my attention to the lateness of the day, and the fact that I had no torch ("won't need one, won't be home late...") Instantly I flew into 'gotta get outta here' mode. Time to get the fish home and claim my beery bounty – unless of course my challenger had caught a fish sooner, or a larger one simultaneously. Both eventualities were highly unlikely. I had the bet in a box. I headed for the user-unfriendly path back home.

Before I got to the base of the hill, I stopped and wondered – would I make it back to the motorbike before dark? If I headed straight up the hill here instead of going on to the known path, the walk would be shorter – but only *if* I could get myself and the fishing gear through the bush, which though extensive, looked sparse enough to let me through.

"Should I, shouldn't I? Should I, shouldn't I?"

I did, and about half way up I knew I shouldn't have. I wasn't going to win *this* fight – I wasn't going any further upward in any direction. I was also carrying far more weight than when I had come down – the source of which, obviously, I was happy about and had no intention of jettisoning. (Nor of course, as per usual, did I have any drinking water that could be jettisoned – or drunk – either!)

With no other option I fought my way back down again and clambered along the rocky walk to the base of the hill, where in rapidly diminishing light I launched my assault on the steep but known path back home. With some relief, as it was pitch black by then, I reached my trusty bike. By the time I got home, 'cracker safely in pannier, rods on crash bars and other equipment attached to my body by whatever means possible, I was back in an elated state again. My adversary – the beer-betting one – was an honourable chap and must have anticipated defeat because soon I was sucking on my prize – *without* any sea watery type of reaction!

Some years after this I was again challenged to a bet – with bigger stakes for a far bigger fish, by a far less honourable loser. More on this later…

Chapter 4

The George Days: High Cliffs, Wild Seas, Big Fish, Rotten Bait, a Second Wager and a Lot More

When I first arrived in George, I hopped on the BMW and launched a 'reconnaissance assault' on the area's *very* impressive coastline. Beach after beautiful beach lay hidden amongst massive rocky cliffs. Headlands dropped sheer into deep, wild water, while lush green hills and trees formed a friendly background right up to the base of the mighty Outeniqua Mountain range. The mountains themselves towered into the sky almost like a benevolent God overseeing the magical greens, subtle mauves and pastel blues of the rolling hills. These contrasted strongly against the mountain, whilst its own outline contrasted even more strikingly against the sky. *SHEEESH*, it was beautiful! For a while I just stood there and allowed myself to get lost in the landscape.

Eventually a pounding heart brought me back to myself and my mission. At last I had access to raw, rugged, challenging water at its best. I could *sense* big fish down there, beckoning.

Left: *A good day for fishing.*

Right: *A bad day for fishing. Very different conditions at the same spot, looking south from Rooikrantz, near Roodekrantz, close to the town of George on the eastern Cape coast of South Africa.*

The urge to pit myself against big fish in a fair duel had been with me since I could remember – the larger the fish, the better. I thought once again with some amusement of the easier avenue of boat fishing, especially the manner in which the fighting and landing of some big game fish is conducted:

"This is getting a bit too much for me old chap, keep spilling my bloody gin. Won't you just reverse the boat so the bloody fish doesn't pull so damned hard? There's a good fellow. *Watch* out, you'll cut the line, *swing around* you bloody fool! By George that was close. Actually someone else can take over – I've had e'bloody nuff! Give me a hand out of this infernal chair, Walter. Blimey, I need to go on a bloody diet. Another gin please."

Ever try telling solid rock to reverse for your convenience, or asking the shellfish not to cut your line? No. (Well, you might have in a desperate moment but it wouldn't have helped much. Rock anglers tend to pray more than demand.) And therein lies the challenge – you do it right yourself, or you pay. Which is what, in my humble opinion, makes rock fishermen the elite of the fishing fraternity.

Back to George. One fishing spot in the area towered above the rest in magnitude and magnificence – remote, high-cliffed, very deep and very difficult – indeed potentially dangerous when it came to actually landing a fish. This was George's Roodekrantz, familiar to relatively few of the fishing fraternity – only the crazed fanatics. Incidentally, for the benefit of English speakers and

Aussies, Roodekrantz is not pronounced 'Rude-crantz' even if it looks as though it should be. It is actually closer to Roo-udder-crar-n-tz. (Well, sort of.) The names of sacred fishing places deserve the effort.

Over time I grew to love the place. On rough, wild and windy days I would simply ride down on the BM, sit on the cliff top, and become absorbed in those mysterious depths. I was always curious to see if a swell big enough to churn the sand in front of Roodekrantz would turn up while I was there, but it never did. At that depth the waves never broke – the water was reputed by divers to be 60 feet deep right in front of the rocks, and judging by the time it took for a heavy sinker to hit bottom, it was. Roodekrantz became a part of my life for which I would definitely appreciate a replay button.

Above: *Roodekrantz. 60 ft of incredible water – straight off the front!*

I had known the instant I saw it that there would be big fish there – but that not many would have been captured. I also knew instantly that I would acquaint myself with Roodekrantz and its lesser (though still impressive) surrounds – the surrounds being kept in reserve for whenever an even slightly troubled sea rendered Roodekrantz itself out of bounds.

For a long time Roode and its neighbouring spots delivered only relatively small fish, as if they were knowingly restricting me to a familiarisation period. These fish could all be lifted up the high rocks without gaffing, provided the line was strong enough. I never used less than 40lb line in these areas and still lost fish. Catches consisted mainly of the eastern Hottentot (*Pachymetopon grande*) with an occasional galjoen (*Coracinus capensis*) or wildeperd (zebrafish, *Diplodus trifasciatus*), the latter more common when persistent south easterly winds put a chill in the water. I also landed the occasional musselcracker in the area, but they generally favoured shallower terrain.

Incidentally, the Hottentot's name, like so many other fish names, is a little puzzling. The name was originally given to an indigenous tribe of South Africa, well known for the sound of its spoken language – a language liberally interspersed with clicks, clacks, the occasional cluck, and presumably also some hots and tots. All well and good. However, while I have heard many a fish grunt – hardly surprisingly their capture tends to bring it on – in all my years I have never been privy to a fish either 'hotting' or 'totting'. Never.

Perhaps also a little hard to explain – or perhaps even to believe – is something I first read about in S. Schoeman's superb book *'Strike!'* This fact is, however, strongly supported by word of mouth, and I have since experienced it many times myself. All of the above species have a strong penchant for rock or redbait (conjevoi to some). Not, mind you, only in the fresh state that even humans eat it, presumably to stave off death by starvation. Fish liking the fresh stuff wouldn't be surprising. No, these strange fish prefer it rotten. Again, not just rotten, but **ROTTEN!** Rotten to the extent of losing its red colour – whitening or slightly bluing in a good batch – and fast approaching liquid form. To give a helpful comparison, snot and raw oysters, apart from their different smell and colour, are uncannily similar, in texture at least. But the smell…Hooboy! One could surmise that it is not so much a fondness on the part of the fish that seems to call them in droves, but rather that its fragrance is of such phenomenal magnitude that every fish for miles around approaches out of curiosity. Quite simply, it stinks to high heaven.

But no, the evidence that they actually do love to eat it is overwhelming. There are few baits that will elicit the kind of attack that this slimy, stinky mucus will. Whenever I used it there was usually no need, or even opportunity, to strike to set the hook. The fish's crazed 'hit and run' did it all. I never wedged my rod into the rocks and walked away when using this bait – it was simply too fast and the attacks too powerful to take the risk. Baits are sometimes referred to as fast or slow depending on how long it is likely to take before they attract an enquiry, and also upon how long the bait is likely to withstand the onslaught of small fish, referred to as 'peckers' or 'bait robbers'. Crabs, live-bait and octopus are slow baits, likely to attract bigger fish, and resistant to pecker-attack, while prawns, worms, 'pillies' and redbait are fast; usually, but not only, rapidly attracting smaller fish which are also more plentiful. Being soft, these baits can be stripped off the hook in seconds.

On this scale of fast or slow, rotten redbait fluctuates between supersonic and the speed of light. It probably depends on how much actual bait remains on the hook and how much is just the odour lingering on the copious amounts of elastic 'tie-on' cotton (very much needed to keep it on the hook) after ninety percent of the bait is lost in the cast. Whichever it is, they go for it in a big way.

Above, next page: *These catches are testaments to the power of rotten redbait – most were captured thanks to it.*

Left: *Note the 6 lb wildeperd (the striped fish) in the photo.*

A typical trip to this high-rocked area was not a simple matter, especially in the late spring and early summer when musselcracker would also be on the target list. The others tended to be more winter fare, but there was an overlap. A trip covering both – which was certainly preferable considering the long and arduous trek to get there – would entail a considerable amount of effort, including preparation.

Bait had to be gathered. Rotten redbait could be created by a slow maturation process but I was never on sufficiently good terms with the neighbours and chose rather to collect the pulpy pods some time after they had been dislodged from their rocky purchase by rough seas. They would wash around for some time before becoming wedged amongst exposed rocks or coming to rest above the high tide mark on beaches, deposited there by obliging currents. 'Ripeness' was evidenced by a distinct physical change from the fresh, hard, rough, red-brown outer case to a softer, smoother case which became pulpy and grey-brown, with slimy white-grey areas at the feeding apertures; the softer, greyer and pulpier the better. If trodden on they would emit a jet of viscous fluid whose odour defies description.

I *could* tell the story of a certain Englishman, one David Liversage, (a name easily remembered as he would complain about people calling him Liversausage) who accompanied me one day out of curiosity in search of this unbelievable bait. On this occasion, a very large, ripe redbait pod, inadvertently trodden on by myself, doused him copiously in a horrific direct-experience of the offensive stuff.

The co-incidences surrounding the event (the size and ripeness of the pod, the accuracy of the jet and its generous volume) have prompted some to raise an eyebrow at the claim of 'inadvertence', but I just don't have that sort of sense of humour...

(I *could* tell the story – but won't in case he still wants to kill me.)

So much for the collection of old redbait which was then cut from the pod and kept in a small, very well sealed plastic bucket. If the rotten stuff was unavailable, fresh redbait would be pulled from the rocks at low tide with a gaff, or better still a double hooked bait-hook on a long bamboo pole. The process almost invariably involved wave-dodging and precarious rock hopping. In more recent times this practice has been replaced by the more conservation-oriented practice of cutting the bait out and leaving the empty shell in place. I am not sure how this improves the bait's re-growth prospects as the old pod must then rot off before new redbait larvae (or other organisms) can settle on the spot and grow. Nevertheless, effective efforts at conservation are essential, and should, in principle and practice, be welcomed and supported.

The collection of bait crabs has been described. The next stage in the fishing trip would be preparation of fishing tackle in readiness for an early start, and the step after that, the early start itself. When fishing for musselcracker at usually remote and hard-to-access spots, this would mean very early indeed – up in the dark. A loud alarm clock placed on the other side of the bedroom would force a full-bodied evacuation from the bed, thereby eliminating the possibility of switching the alarm off and drifting back to sleep again.

Now for some inexplicable reason there seems to be *no* aspect of this sport which isn't susceptible to interruptions to its smooth progression. In the case of getting up early this took the form of occasional failure to do so, despite my best efforts.

With bitter experience having resulted in most other possible causes of failure to rise being eliminated, one remaining trouble-maker was the weather. An evening of relentlessly howling wind and pounding rain would occasionally dampen my spirits to the point of acknowledging that the situation was hopeless. I would accept defeat and go to bed without a primed alarm clock. The shock of then being awakened by a smiling sun on a beautiful windless, cloudless, post-storm Saturday morning, having missed my opportunity, would be almost too much to bear. My error of judgement would be painful almost to the point of wearing black for several days.

"So what?" you ask. "What's one day, for pity's sake?"

What sad ignorance. Only a non-fisherperson would ever ask. Let me explain the blatantly obvious. There are only so many days on which one is free to fish. There are only so many days of good weather. There are only so many days in the fishes' season which have suitable tides. And there is tragically little overlap. These days are *precious!*

However, if all such obstacles were overcome, and providing I was not depending on a clapped-out old beach buggy – as I did for a brief period of time – I would be seaward-bound. After a twenty to thirty minute drive, the last part of which was often on atrocious dirt track, I would arrive at the end of the easy part. Almost invariably a long walk including a stiff, sometimes quite difficult climb or rocky clamber – usually by torchlight carrying a heavy back-pack and cumbersome bundle of rods and gaff – would follow. At last, often only as the first signs of dawn appeared, the spot would be reached and the state of the sea could be assessed.

As fast as could be managed, but with attention to the need for good knots, sharp hooks and carefully attached bait, the first rig would be prepared. As soon as there was sufficient daylight, this was sent on its mission by a mighty hoist heavenwards. Thereafter there was time to relax, find a rock that best agreed with the shape of one's backside, and allow the soul to soak up the magic of fishing while the sun rose.

On a good day, even using crab for bait, the wait could be short – not even long enough for a numbing of the butt – before the crab would be found by an early hunter and all hell would break loose. That was, of course, unless they were being sly and picky, as even the biggest brutes can be when it suits them. But this was often an intense period of fish-feeding – the best time of the day – responded to by considerable efforts on my part to exploit it by minimising the periods of 'no bait in the water'. The time could be hectic indeed.

On a bad day the only joy would be the place and the sea, and the fact that I wasn't at work – not that any of these should be undervalued. The fish would either have vacated the area for better hunting grounds or they would be on hunger strike. Either way it would be dead. Hour after hour it would be a matter of changing baits, trying different strategies, watching the sun rise and tides change. Changing of venues was also an option, and not being a lazy angler, I did so as often as I deemed necessary. The decision-making and procrastination over the merits of the different options threatened to drive me crazy. The best choice was *so* important, but how could one be *sure*? It was all taken rather seriously!

On one such occasion the decision had been made to move. Musselcracker season was in full swing and I was hell bent on making the most of it. The exact spot I was fishing was new to me, though I knew the general area well – or so I thought. A possible short-cut existed up a thirty metre near-vertical rock-face, which despite being so steep, was kind enough to have plenty of ledges to stand on, and a craggy surface offering easy hand holds, overall looking moderately difficult but quite do-able. Time was of the essence and up I went. Up and up......and up. Not quickly, but steadily, until with some relief I approached the top. Then all of a sudden I found myself unable to proceed. An overhang not evident in my initial survey blocked my way. Sideways movement was also out of the question. Shit! Prime fishing time was slipping by.

Down was the only possible direction, but even this was not easy. I was holding on with one hand and couldn't turn, as I needed to, without taking off my backpack. I was also holding onto two large heavy rods, a slightly lighter one and a long gaff. Holding the rods between my chest and the rock-face, I very carefully manoeuvred the bag off my back and placed it on the very narrow ledge I was standing on then turned my attention to downward movement once more. As I did so, I either bumped the bag, or its contents shifted, and horror of horrors, down it fell, spinning and bumping as it went, to crash horribly onto the rocks below and end up most uncomfortably close to the sea itself. Double shit! Bagless and hence somewhat 'enlightened', albeit it not in the preferred manner, I made my way gloomily back down and retrieved the bag. The event was such that the details are well remembered to this day. The bag contained, amongst other things:

1. Two Penn 49 'A' reels and a Penn 500 Jigmaster;
2. A plastic bucket holding at least six (hard earned) rock crabs;
3. Very unusually, an old (and cheap) instamatic camera;
4. Even more unusually, a one litre plastic bottle of water. (Obviously I had learned to carry water by then – well at least sometimes); and
5. Three apples in a Styrofoam tray with cling wrap. (Food - also very rare.)

The rest was unbreakable: heavy sinkers, hooks, swivels, knife etc. Of all the above contents, the reels and camera survived totally unscathed. *Every* crab was destroyed – totally unusable. All three apples were smashed and the water bottle was holed. Incredible but true. Neptune was obviously asleep or *everything* would have been 'vlenters'. (Afrikaans for 'smashed to pieces' in this context.)

The lack of crabs for bait meant that my musselcracker opportunities were as dashed as the crabs were. It was high tide and I was unable to capture any more crabs, or scrounge any other kind of bait. I went home.

On a less disastrous day I would move from site to site, settling in if one showed promise, but moving on if that felt right; up rocks, down rocks, through bush and over hills. Eventually as the day wore on it would become evident that no further action was likely and the day's efforts could be drawn to a halt. Sometimes there would be some pressing need to go home at a particular time, which fact, as any serious fisherman will acknowledge, is somehow known to fish, prompting them to mysteriously come on the bite just moments before one has to leave.

If fish had been caught, the haul home could be heavy going. Big fish are not easy to carry, and carrying more than one can be extremely awkward. They flop about, depositing slime and slipping off whatever equipment had been improvised to secure them. For example, if two large fish of say 20 lbs each had been captured, I would tie their jaws together and sling them over my shoulder, one in front, one behind. After twenty minutes, this slippery mass sliding around one's shoulders and body, flopping wetly backwards and forwards and causing the connecting rope to dig into one, could become extremely tiring and tiresome. Being spiked by a fin spine or two wouldn't help matters either. Half to three quarter hour walks and longer were commonplace. Rests would be frequent and sweat profuse. However, arriving back at the vehicle, handing the transportation duty over to it, and getting back home victorious and triumphant, was 'as sweet as'.

The last energy to be exerted would be in photographing and cleaning the fish, if it (or they) had not already been cleaned at the sea. Cleaning the fish at the fishing site was very rarely done as photographs needed to be taken while the fish was still intact and looking good. Weighing however, was better done immediately, before precious weight (for records and story-telling purposes) could be lost by way of dripping, evaporation, a post mortem piss, poop or whatever. Hence my preference for always carrying a scale with me, but only very occasionally a camera – fishing duty was a bit rough on cameras, to say the least. Cameras needed to function perfectly but a slightly rusted scale spring (provided it increased the weight and didn't decrease it – heaven forbid) was never a problem. Anyway, most fish were carried back to home or campsite intact.

Getting back to Roodekrantz, any place that I fished so frequently simply had to produce a hook-in-the-body-story – and Roodekrantz certainly did. The hook was a small one but it got stuck in a very inconvenient place. No not *there* – I *knew* you would think that! No, this hook got me in the mouth, which was nearly as bad. Well, maybe not. But it was bad enough.

The intention at the time was to catch some live-bait, and I was trying to fasten a very small hook to some heavier line than I should have been using for the purpose. I was battling to tighten the knot. It kept springing loose (the way they do) and even the application of loud bad language wasn't helping. Eventually in a fit of frustrated impatience I took the hook between my teeth and hauled on the line. Of *course* it slipped and, "OH, HHPHUCK!" the hook embedded itself on the inside of my lower lip. (Hence the strange pronunciation. *You* try and say the word with a hook in your inner lower lip.)

So there I was, in another of those strange dilemmas. Fortunately there was no chance of curious observers gawking as very few people fished the place. The hook was in beyond the barb, and I was in a new kind of relationship with my fishing rod. What to do? I carried the rod (carefully) over to my fishing bag where, fortunately, I had some pliers. Cutting the line with a knife would have produced some very uncomfortable sensations on my lip via the hook. A fisherman learns these facts of life as a matter of course.

Once I had managed to wrench open the rusted jaws of the pliers I was at least able to cut off the eye of the hook, and hence also the line, thus severing the relationship with the rod. I knew I would then either have to go home – most annoying – or remove the hook forwards, which anyone knowing the actual toughness of the lower lip will testify would not be easy. Its soft floppiness is *very* deceptive – if you don't believe me, take a small hook on some fishing line and…oh never mind – just trust me.

Try as I might, I could not extend my eyeballs and lower lip far enough to actually see the hook, though I came close. Not only is the lower lip tough, but it will stretch quite impressively when obliged, but not sufficiently so on that occasion. So I had to work blind, trying to get a grip on the tiny hook with a pair of pliers whose jaws were so severely rusted that they could not easily find purchase on something so small.

I will cut a long, complicated and saliva-dripping-from-mouth story short, and just say that somehow I did eventually manage to get a grip on the hook, and with a quick, vigorous, and eye-watering twist, managed to push the barb through forwards. Then, with a final easy pull with the fingertips, out it came. Whew, what a relief! Once again Neptune had had his revenge on behalf of the fishes.

Left: *Hook in the lip - one of many hook-in-the-body episodes.*

A final story involving Roodekrantz can be told before moving on. This is the tale of the bad wager referred to earlier. There was, in the town of George, a particular café, which apart from the usual café fare, stocked an excellent range of fishing tackle. I was a good customer even if many of the larger items I purchased, such as fishing rods, were second hand. (Young bachelor – no money.) The proprietors were well known for being amongst the very few fishermen who had fished Roodekrantz, and even fewer who, in times gone by, had caught the famed large poensies (black steenbras) that frequented the area. I asked about the place saying that I too wished to wet a line there with this in mind.

The owner looked at me scornfully.

"HHUUMMPPH! I'll give you a thousand metres of line if you catch a poensie there – if you don't drown."

"What sort of line?" I asked, becoming interested.

"Won't make any difference, those poensies are something else. Ah well, 60 lb. That's what you'll need there. What are you using, 20 lb huh? Scoff, scoff."

"Nope, 60 lb. What size poensie do I need?" I asked this to ensure that a size was settled upon so there were no moveable goalposts, even if there were unfortunately no witnesses present at the time.

"At least 40 lb! Guffaw, guffaw, scoff, scoff, snort!"

His mockery did him no good service, just made me more determined – if that was possible.

I may have tried a few times on my own before *the* day, but on *the* day, 2/1/1974, I was accompanied to

Roodekrantz by two very accomplished rock fishermen, Johan Terblanche and Johan Westenraad. (Johan Terblanche was the fisherman I had beaten to catch the first musselcracker of the season in the earlier betting story.) The sea was magnificent and calm, as it needed to be. We fished the morning at a spot to the side of Roodekrantz called Rooikrantz, also very deep water. Sometime that morning Johan T. hooked a large fish, using if I recall correctly, a live 'gorrie' (or pinkie, *Pomadasys olivaceum*) for bait. This was a common little fish which made a grunting sound when caught but was not usually used alive unless better options were unavailable.

Anyway a large fish found it palatable, swallowed it, got hooked, and gave Johan stick. He eventually turned and held it, and finally started recovering line. The next problem was where and how to land it. This was a near impossibility. As so often happens to fishermen, he had hooked a larger than expected fish when circumstances were against him. There was simply nowhere to bring it to the gaff. (Most surprisingly Johan had apparently not surveyed the area for this very factor in advance.) He had no option but to try to manoeuvre the fish up the sheer rock and hope the line didn't break before it could be reached with a gaff – and this was potentially an extremely difficult and dangerous gaffing job which Johan would not have expected us to attempt too far down the long and near vertical rock face.

The degree of success which he achieved in lifting the fish before it broke loose and fell back was remarkable, as it was large and still flapping, but it was far from the reach of the gaff. Interestingly it was the hook which broke and not the line. The fish was a poensie and Johan must have been horribly disappointed. These fish are scarce, extremely hard and dirty fighters, and are rightly considered to be a prize catch. Well, we knew they were about anyway. Johan W. had to leave but fortunately Johan T. and I were able to stay on. We decided to move around the corner to Roodekrantz itself. It was a beautiful, calm, sunny day and the sea lapped passively against the orange/red rock below. Perfect for finding poensies and for getting them out.

Roode was a better spot in terms of gaffing options than Rooikrantz. What that meant is that it was only bloody difficult, not totally impossible. One could fish comfortably and safely enough from a high, reasonably level rocky area perhaps fifteen metres in length. A large concrete block had been built onto it for some reason unknown to me, possibly military. It would certainly have made a good vantage point. The front of that rocky ledge dropped four or so metres vertically to another ledge below of about the same length, perhaps three or four metres wide and close to sea level, the actual drop to the sea depending on the tide.

This lower ledge was accessible from either side of the fishing ledge but only with difficulty. Apart from the awkward access and the fact that even a slight swell in the deep water could lift over and swamp it totally, the ledge was a good gaffing site, but one to be used with enormous care.

We set about catching some live-bait. It seemed incongruous to be throwing a light rig into these great depths looking for small fish, waiting for ages for the sinker to hit the bottom. Catching live-bait can vary between very easy and impossible, more commonly tending towards the latter, with limitless degrees of frustration in between, mostly extreme. (Of course, the time when you only manage to catch a single precious live-bait is the very time a seagull is most likely to come along and steal the thing out of its rock pool before you can tackle up for it…) I got lucky that day and quite soon, after a tell-tale enthusiastic 'tak, tak, tak' of a bite, I hooked and landed a suitably sized karanteen or strepie (*Sarpa salpa*) around 20 cm in length. You *beauty*! Seconds later (I wasn't game to risk losing it to a bird while I fished for another one) out it went, a 6/0 or 7/0 short-shank Mustad Beak hook securing it, and 60 lb Maxima line ensuring we kept in contact.

The trap was set, now for the wait. As was my habit, I held the rod for perhaps twenty minutes before acknowledging that the prey was not immediately at hand, then propped it into a gap in the rocks, making absolutely sure it was securely wedged and the drag set extremely lightly with ratchet engaged. I then sat back comfortably. The outfit I was using was a trusty old Penn 49 'A' reel and a Silaflex fishing rod given to me by my father. With both rod and reel being experienced veterans, I knew I could trust them to do their share in any battle.

I recall that, as was so often the case, I had dozed off lightly but delectably when the reel screamed. As always, when the reel screamed I was shocked back to consciousness at lightning speed by a near heart attack. I leapt over, disengaged the ratchet to avoid scaring the fish off, freed the spool and allowed the fish to run. Simultaneously I worked the rod free from the rocks, lifted it and faced it towards the fish, sloping down slightly to minimize line resistance and position it for a strike. How long to let it run? Too long and it might drop the bait. Too short and it might not have swallowed it. This is always a difficult decision, and one that can never be made with certainty. I have had fish run for what seemed like ages only to strike and pull the bait from their mouths with hardly a mark on it. *Very* frustrating.

Already shaking, I tightened the drag, engaged the spool, and waited for the fish to take up the slack, which it did in no uncertain terms. Hit one! Solid. *IN!* Hit two! Solid! Hit three! Solid! Hit four! Hit five! I didn't hold back. It is too easy to miss a live-bait pick-up for several reasons. The hook can easily twist back such that its point is hidden in the bait. Furthermore poensies, if that's what it was, have jaws akin to stone and a mouth full of pebble-like teeth, so the hook is not easy to set. Finally, they will make for the rocks at the slightest hint of an opportunity – and they are usually strong enough to make their own opportunities. I first watched an East London wall fisherman strike like this and thought to myself, "Is that really necessary?" Then I lost a few big fish on live-bait and got my answer. Nowadays with big fish off the rocks I don't take chances. I strike with intent.

This fish, big as it was, didn't get an opportunity to turn and go. I kept pumping repeatedly, and winding when I could, each pump almost a strike but now longer, slower and more sustained in the upward haul, winding on the down-movement. If it took line at all it didn't get much. I maintained high pressure at the risk of a broken line – believe me even sixty pound line can break all too easily under this pressure.

I steadily worked my quarry up from the depths, still not knowing what it was, praying it was something good but knowing it could very easily be a shark even though I wasn't using a steel trace. Already Johan was waiting, his own line retrieved, gaff at the ready, watching my progress. (As I said, he's a good fisherman.) Haul, wind, shake! Haul, wind, shake! I was shaking with exertion, anticipation and fear of loss all at once. That's a bucket-load of shake and it showed. This continued without variation until, all of a sudden, the fish broke the surface.

"OH MY GOD – IT'S A POENSIE" were my actual words as my brain registered with shock and joy that one of my greatest angling dreams could soon be realized. Johan had already leapt past behind me and spider-manned his way at blinding pace down the rock wall to the gaffing ledge. In one continuous flowing movement he reached the edge, swung the gaff, hooked solidly, and seemingly effortlessly lifted the enormous fish. He ran to the opposite end of the ledge and made his way up the steep rock to where I was waiting. It was an incredible piece of gaffing, the likes of which I will probably never see again. I

sincerely hope he gets to read these words in published form and to know that my gratitude has never diminished.

I, in the meantime, had had to sit down. My legs had said 'enough already' and I had no option but to obey them. I looked at my prize from a sitting position. Any view would have been fantastic. After recovering my composure somewhat, it dawned on me that I might have a specimen which satisfied the requirements of my wager. It looked to be within reach of forty pounds, but only a scale could confirm this. A thousand metres of line would be very handy, thank you.

Neither of us had a scale with us, but it was in any case the café man's scale that would do the official reading. (You could bet on *that*!) I needed to get the fish there before it lost too much weight. I wasn't taking any chances. As it turned out, despite the fact that Johan kindly carried my fishing rods, it was I who lost weight on the way home, not the fish. If you have ever carried such a large fish uphill for twenty minutes you will know why. The day was still warm and I poured with perspiration.

We went straight home. Johan had to leave and only stayed long enough for our own 'weigh in'. The scale went willingly to 40 lb but not a poofteenth of an ounce over. What would the Café man's own scale say? The spring of *his* scale would certainly not be rusty – strengthened more likely. Johan left and without delay I loaded the fish and headed, full of anticipation, in the direction of the café, and hopefully lots of lovely fishing line.

I entered the shop right in view of the proprietor, carrying my prize. From memory it may have been around two months since the bet had been forged. He grudgingly acknowledged my fish, weighed it and put it at forty pounds. I waited for further comment. None was forthcoming. I was a little taken aback. The undertaking hadn't been vague, made in haste, or taken place too long before. I attempted to jog his memory. It was strange, he barely seemed to recognize me, let alone recall any bet. I told him the details of our conversation. Eventually, while still denying any memory of it, he agreed to give me a few hundred metres of a lower breaking strain line. Apart from any other consideration, I would have thought that the good publicity from an honoured bet would have been worth more in business terms than the negative impact produced by his denials. The line wouldn't have cost him that much. No matter, I'm an angler not a gambler.

Left: *A rare photograph of the author wearing a tie, taken the day after the catch was made, holding the 40 lb poensie in the bet.*

Left: *Jaws like stone – showing the poensie's teeth. The head was preserved by injecting it with formaldehyde. It was never allowed in the lounge room of the communal house, but after some months it was sneaked into my bedroom where it lived in the good company of other angling-related smells.*

Talking of Johan T. ('the gaffer') brings back memories of another event in which I didn't end up being so happy with him – more like substantially pissed off. It also reminds me how the risks in rock fishing lie not only in rocks and sea. We had been contemplating a trip south of Mossel Bay, perhaps as far as Ystervarkfontein. I first visited Ystervarkfontein out of curiosity. The name literally means 'Iron pig fountain'. A FOUNTAIN OF IRON PIGS? I felt like ducking every time I saw a suspicious shadow.

We eventually decided on something closer and arose very early one weekend morning – long before the sparrows had even finished digesting their evening meal let alone started farting from it. In the pitch dark we drove from George through Mossel Bay to that beautiful natural rocky breakwater at Fransmanshoek. In that magnificent area we fished dark into daylight, daylight into midday, midday into afternoon and afternoon back into darkness, with only a shark or two for our efforts. One of these was hungry enough to bite Johan's trace off and get caught again not too long afterwards, still trailing the original trace and sinker from its mouth.

Whatever pain and fear fish experience, they certainly have a remarkable capacity for ignoring it. I myself have on several occasions lost fish which have then taken a bait almost immediately thereafter and been hooked a second time, with the first trace still in their mouths. I most certainly do not have the same capacity to forget a bad fright. I tend to remember it for years…

Having fished ourselves to a standstill, Johan and I realized with our usual reluctance that our time was up. The night had already reached middle age and we needed to get home before close relatives started to think that maybe we weren't coming home at all. (In those days that wonderful aid in such situations, the mobile telephone, was still waiting to be invented.) We packed up, loaded his faithful Volkswagen Beetle, and hit the road. We were knackered, but I at least had the option of snoozing; or so I believed. I couldn't help myself anyway. My head nodded within minutes.

Then: "Wake up! Talk to me!" Johan pushed my shoulder roughly. He needed my help to stay awake. It was certainly in my interest to do so, but more easily asked for than achieved. I nodded off again within seconds. Johan was obviously having the same problem, which was making driving tricky. Quite understandably, he appealed to me again.

"Man, *FUCK* you! Stay awake you *bastard* – you think you can sleep while I have to drive? Talk to me! Sing! Shout! *DON'T* fall afuckingsleep!"

I could tell he was serious, but I was powerless and after mumbling something that would have been more likely to bore him to death, I nodded off again. Mistake! I don't know how long it was before it happened, as I was sound asleep. I was jerked awake by a combination of ultra-powerful waking agents: my head smacked into the dashboard / the Beetle was in a four wheeled drift on dirt, tyres roaring, dust billowing / trees were racing to meet us /

Johan was screaming at the top of his voice, "EEEEEEAAAAAAAAHHHH…"

I joined in with a loud, "SHIT! *FUUUU- U – U – U – U – U...*"

In mid 'fuuuuuu' I felt the car swing around away from the trees and slow down, tyres spinning normally, then grind to a halt.

"*NOW* will you STAY AWAKE?" Johan was glaring at me, but also chuckling heartily. Sonofabitch, the bastard had done it on purpose. I stayed awake then. I couldn't sleep with my eyes open, and I doubt whether I even blinked them for the rest of the trip. I was also talking as requested, but so rapidly that the frequency would only have been audible to a dog. Johan didn't complain – maybe he could hear it. Anyway, he was too busy laughing in great bellows that would occasionally diminish then find new life as he recalled the event. I sat rigid, 'penregop' (rigidly upright) – hair included – for the rest of the trip. Fish may forget a fright but I am not so fortunate.

Then there was the matter of the infamous beach buggy (pictured on page 81, on one of its few functional days). Some time after I arrived in George I decided that the place was so promising as a fishing venue that my bike might one day be overwhelmed by demands on its carrying capacity – which is actually a good kind of problem if you think about it.

Above: *I didn't forget a scary event as quickly as fish seem to…*

At about the same time it came to my attention that someone at work had a beach buggy to sell. Word was that it was 'not a bad buy' (better for a liar's conscience than saying 'it's a good buy'), being cheap and quite experienced in angling matters.

A further strong selling point was its state of repair. Its valuable fishing experience had rendered its appearance such that if you added any scratches, scrapes, dents or holes, or acquired more rust on the chassis, you wouldn't notice the difference and feel bad. Yes, I could appreciate that – a distinct plus. So I bought it and became the proud owner of my first four-wheeled vehicle. Not 4 wheel drive mind you, just four wheels. That I ever actually went anywhere with it (not to mention coming back) is a mixture of good luck and the fact that I had lots of friends who wanted to go fishing but did not wish to wreck their own vehicles in the salty environment. A little pushing – even a lot – was a reasonable price to pay to avoid using one's own car.

This was an otherwise sort of a vehicle – clearly possessing its own very contrary consciousness. I was told (sometime *after* I purchased it, of course) that it had on at least one occasion come close to being drowned in sea water. I suppose some talented sales person could even have put a positive slant on *that*. In any case, the result was a very faulty electrical system. On a good night its lights would malfunction, on a bad night they wouldn't function at all. When it was cold it was extremely difficult to start. When it was hot it was impossible to start.

Leaving it running for an entire fishing trip was out of the question, though it certainly crossed my mind considering how long it took to start it in the first place. Interestingly, I quickly came to the realization that the availability of long downhill slopes, at the top of which the buggy might be parked for starting purposes, was inversely proportional to the degree of remoteness of the fishing spot.

The BMW bike was far more reliable, probably drier in the rain as there was nothing on it to actually channel the rain onto one, and it carried more fish than the buggy. Not that it had a greater carrying capacity. It didn't. It was just more capable of getting to the fishing spots and back again.

It finally dawned on me that the buggy's totally non-starting days were the best days I had with it. After bogging, breaking down, or losing my lights on one occasion too many, I got rid of it.

Above: *The infamous open-sided 'Purple Peril' or 'Mauve Monster' beach buggy, depending on what one would have called its delightful colour.*

It was either given away gratefully or sold for considerably less than I paid. I can't remember which; the pleasant memories of no longer having it overwhelm any other memories. It did carry a few musselcracker, but nothing which the BM wouldn't have managed to carry with ease. Unfortunately, I have a picture of the buggy and one fish but none of the BM with, for example, a large 'cracker's tail sticking out of its pannier. This had the added distinct advantage of being very visible to onlookers.

Right: *Dave
with a 33 lb
musselcracker.*

Sometime in the George era I was introduced to Robberg at Plettenberg Bay by an old friend and capable fishing buddy, Dave Krebser. He had, amongst other notable catches, landed a 55 lb tuna on a spoon near the Gap on Robberg, and was amply qualified to fill me in on this great peninsula.

The rocky structure of Robberg (meaning seal mountain) protrudes several kilometres out to sea, and is possibly best known to local anglers for the amazing oceanic phenomenon it produces when a strong south easterly wind prevails for several days.

Right: *Dave Krebser's 55 lb Robberg tuna.*

On such occasions, after the wind has blown sufficiently, cold water wells up and moves in towards the coast, pushing marine animals, often plentiful and sometimes very sizeable, ahead of it. These become concentrated in the large bay area formed on the north side of Robberg, in an area of warm water which is contained there. This may last a few days, but a change in wind direction causes cold water to move in rapidly and the fish to move out, thereby ending the action.

I was not fortunate enough to make very many trips under these amazing circumstances but on a few of those that I did make, the results were spectacular. Fish 'for Africa' abounded. Acres of tightly packed bait-fish, huge shoals of garrick (leervis *Lichia amia*), occasional yellowtail (*Seriola lalandi*) up to 50 lb or more, groups of large (and sometimes enormous) tuna of species unknown to me but probably bluefin judging by their size, and sharks and rays of various sizes and types condensed into the area. It was an angler's dream come true.

After a good blow, when circumstances permitted me to get there (public holidays were not declared, though they should have been) I would rise in the dark, or even leave on the afternoon before and walk the approximately three-quarter hour journey to the point. There I would find a sheltered spot amongst some smelly, scrubby bushes, curl up in my clothes, and fall asleep thinking of big fish. No alarm clock was needed. Howling wind, an uneven rocky mattress and occasional showers of rain would guarantee light sleep and frequent waking.

Smelly bushes? Yes, smelly because after several exposures of my leather jacket (the same one I wore to the job interview) to their crushed leaves while I slept on them, the jacket became indelibly impregnated with their characteristic herb-like odour; not unpleasant but extremely strong and persistent. (Only something impressively strong can rise above years of bait smell.) Nothing could remove it. I didn't mind it; in fact I quite enjoyed it. Years later in Australia I encountered a shrub with an identical smell. What memories it brought back. Was it the same species of shrub? I don't know.

After passing the night neither peacefully nor pleasantly, I would arise, body creaking stiffly, gather up my gear, and with headlamp switched on, make my way down the rocky slopes as first light spread revealingly over this intriguing body of water. What had taken place? Would the fish be there? Only light would tell, and I would wait patiently, straining for the first tell-tale signs.

As it grew light enough to see what I was doing, impatience would take over and I would hurl an investigatory tin spoon (lure) out into the distance in the hope of an early breakfast seeker. Unlike the Transkei coast, this area never yielded – to me at least – anything more than a shad or two in this pre-sunrise period. If I did catch suitably sized shad they most certainly went the same way as the karanteen at Roodekrantz – out to sea as live-bait. I would engage their services post haste provided they were not too big, a pound or so being perfect. It seems only a live shad or similar delectable live offering would tempt the more worthwhile predators so early in the morning.

There was another fascinating phenomenon about the game fish at Robberg. They sometimes appeared in enormous numbers, especially leervis (*Lichia amia*), on my visits; dense enough to bump them with a spoon. But they wouldn't grab at it. Do what you might, they just weren't eating tin at that particular time. *Very* frustrating it was. However, at some time during the morning their brains would jump into feeding gear and one would be hard pressed to retrieve a spoon all the way *without* a hit. It was incredible.

I remember an event in 1982 which involved both the cold water phenomenon *and* that of fish coming on the feed just as I had to leave. After the usual early arrival, I had caught just two leervis after hours of spoon-throwing

..... *THEIR BRAINS WOULD JUMP INTO FEEDING GEAR* ......

during which these two fish had grabbed my spoon, apparently more out of irritation than hunger.

No one else had caught any. My own success was due to blind refusal to give up rather than skill. I worked myself to a frazzle while everyone else just said, "We aren't going to kill ourselves; we'll just watch you until they come on the bite." Well they hadn't come on the bite by the time I had to leave at 9.00 am for a meeting at work at 11.00 am. (A meeting at work – can you believe it!)

As I was leaving I chanced to bump into the local ranger, an occasional acquaintance who included amongst his duties frequent monitoring of local fish stocks, using a fishing rod. This time he had surprisingly left his research equipment at home, and as I would no longer be needing my gear, I offered him my rod, reel and some spoons. Then I left with a sunken heart, knowing the chances were good that the fish would come on the bite some time later.

Sure enough, when he returned my gear that night he said casually, "Pity you had to leave. The leervis went mad. We were having competitions to see who could get their spoon back without hooking one. You take your work too seriously, you know. You would have loved it!" (Thanks for telling me, I would never have guessed.) As if to rub salt in the wound, he pointed to the back of his vehicle. He had kept three fish of about 15 to 18 lb. Obviously his research included palatability tests.

Right: *Two Robberg leervis, or 'garrick' to Natalians.*

Robberg delivered many leervis, and some near misses with large yellowtail and massive tuna. On a number of occasions the latter two species followed my spoon so closely for so long as to produce a fountain of adrenalin from whatever body part makes it, only to leave me gut-wrenchingly disappointed as they turned away at the last moment. A sea of adrenalin would then swirl around my body with no work to do but cause me to shake and utter nasty words.

The place was not only known for game fish. It was good musselcracker territory too. Furthermore, it was quite capable of delivering the unexpected. Over three November days in 1974 it delivered five beautiful fish to me, one of them a rare surprise. I was fishing for musselcracker on the southern side of the peninsula, a little back from the point. Conditions were beautiful: high tide, cloudless and windless, but with a good movement in the sea. At this fairly deep-water spot, this meant that swells would climb up the rocks as high as they could, then plunge back grumpily, not only producing good foamy patches and a 'humpy' water surface, but offering opportunities for lifting big fish progressively higher onto the sloping rocks to land them once they had been pacified sufficiently to do so.

I was using particularly large crabs on that day. Why I'm not sure; perhaps they were the only ones I could catch, but the fact is remembered due to my surprise at catching the unexpected fish on such a big one. Using my Penn 49 'A' and Silaflex combo, I had landed a 14 lb 'cracker to my great delight and was all set to increase my previous record from just one in a day to two. Not long thereafter, down went the rod in a typical 'cracker hit and run – no ifs, buts or maybes. I was into something *really* strong.

As mentioned earlier, on heavy tackle 'cracker do not usually put up a sustained fight. They go very hard initially and then fade. This fish went very hard *without* fading. It tore line off a drag tightened as hard as I could without risking a 'bust up'. I dared not turn the fish by pumping; it would be too easy to push the line over its limit. Surprisingly the fish was heading out rather than sideways or into the rocks as I would have expected of a 'cracker with that sort of strength. This fellow pulled hard, strongly and consistently with a little jerking, not fast and furious like a big enough shark might – not that I expected a shark on a crab bait, but one never knows for sure as strange things happen.

I expected at any moment to feel that terrible rough 'screeking, juddering' (can't come up with better words!) of the line suddenly being pulled around a dreaded rock, one of a rock angler's worst nightmares. Surprisingly, there weren't any rocks out there or the fish was fighting clean; either way it was a huge relief. After some minutes of spectacular and nerve-wracking battle, things slowed down to a more sedate pace – meaning a sort of status quo in which neither the fish nor I gained much ground but in which both parties endeavoured with grim determination to do so.

Eventually, my tackle happily holding out, the fish tired and despite occasional dogged dives and runs I was able to start encouraging it towards the spot in the rocks which had delivered the earlier fish. This was a superbly suitable rock formation for the purpose. A 'V' shape in the rocks, rather like a miniature valley, sloped gently upwards out of the sea from a drop-off into deep water. Incoming swells regularly lifted up and over the steep drop-off, into this cleft, reducing into smaller waves which rushed up into the shallows, enabling a large fish to be pulled progressively closer using these until it was left high and dry. In the prevailing conditions the place was even safe enough for the final capture to be made by hand. Furthermore it was remarkably smooth and free of fouling by mussels or other rock growth. Perfect! There are few things worse than winning a battle to the point of near-victory only to lose a fish at the last moment, especially if there is no confirmatory sighting. Such mishaps leave horrible lingering question marks, the worst of which must surely be whether it was a shark or an edible fish.

Once the fish approached, I was able with surprisingly little difficulty, to use a swell to lift it up out of the depths into the shallower water and then draw it progressively upwards towards me. I couldn't believe my eyes. Though still flapping vigorously, its body was clearly discernible as being much longer and more slender than a 'cracker, and sporting familiar grey bars and an unmistakable big-lipped mouth.

"Crikey – a giant bloody piggy! What a beauty! *Shee-yit!*" The familiar old tremens part of delirium set in as I made the final decisive manocuvres to secure this enormous pignose grunter. Rod still in hand in case of a last-moment disaster, I checked the swell and climbed down to grab it, hand under gill, and clambered up and out again as quickly as possible. No hitches, no bungles. *Fan-tastic!*

That piggy (pignose grunter, *Lithognathus lithognathus*) weighed 31 lb and was my biggest to date. I still hadn't caught two 'cracker in one day, but this was immeasurably better. I need not have worried anyway. For the next two days the weather remained steady and I caught three more musselcracker of 15, 17 and 18 lb, including two on one day. A very happy three days' fishing indeed!

Above: *14 lb musselcracker and 31 lb pignose grunter. Robberg, November 1974.*

To finish off the writings on the southern Cape, there is one episode that came close to terminating that era by almost terminating me. It was my first really close shave with the sea – though not the last. A non-fishing friend had joined me and I was fishing from a rocky promontory situated a few hundred metres south of Roodekrantz.

Above: *15, 18, and 17 lb musselcrackers.*
Robberg, November 1974.

An impression of the nature of the promontory is most easily provided by pointing out that there is a plaque on an overlooking hill commemorating a fisherman who lost his life while fishing from it. From memory, it is perhaps a hundred metres long, rounded at the point, with sides sloping steeply into deep water. On the left, an overhang of rock opposite it creates a progressively narrowing gorge in which waves, after running in from the deep open sea along its side, become constricted. This causes violent churning roaring water and foam, and belches of highly compressed air. It is ugly and would be totally unforgiving to any human body so unfortunate as to find itself swimming in its hellish waters.

On the day in question the water wasn't particularly bad but was nevertheless behaving in a somewhat unpredictable fashion, with sets of bigger waves rolling through periodically. This suggested that a more than usually cautious approach would be prudent. I had hooked a fairly large musselcracker, perhaps 20 lb in weight. Despite my best efforts to persuade it to go right, it decided, with the sea's assistance, to go left, and hence into very difficult landing country. That is to say, it moved into the mouth of the above-mentioned gorge. There would only be one chance at gaffing. The waves would carry the fish with considerable force past me from right to left. It would have to be encouraged as high as possible up the slope as it approached, and then as much holding pressure applied as 50 lb line would allow, while the water receded. Only a reasonably small wave would permit this. My companion was just above me with the gaff which he would pass to me when I called for it. Under the circumstances, I would do the gaffing myself.

The fish was successfully lifted on a suitably sized wave to a position reachable with the gaff. All that was needed was a long enough break between incoming swells to do the job. I was already situated well below the comfort zone and horribly vulnerable. I was handed the gaff and went through the process of positioning it for a strike.

It is probably very fortunate that I was not fast enough to be successful. As they so often do, a large swell arrived just when least needed. It rose up on my right, ominously green, and exploded with an almighty crash as it hit the sloping rock, bursting over it and sweeping along its side towards me. Although a fair distance away, it moved with incredible speed, spreading out to well above me. There was absolutely no time to move out of the way – no alternative but to stay there and hold on – with a large fish still on the line, but fortunately not on the gaff hook.

Realizing my serious predicament with the speed that one does on such occasions, I let go of both rod and gaff, grabbed at the rocks and braced myself just before the wave hit me. It was smaller by then, but still dangerously full of energy despite having initially climbed so high. The gaff disappeared in the maelstrom, but the rod got caught up amongst the rocks and my legs. I heard the 50 lb line break like a pistol shot. Immediately after, I felt my hands start to lose their grip as torrents of water roared down past me – a most horrible feeling. Somehow, despite slipping a short way down, I managed to maintain a purchase which prevented me from being washed into the mouth of the gorge.

As the water passed, I fought my way back up the rocks again, *sans* fish and *sans* gaff, but with something far more precious still intact. (The rod was saved as well.) My companion was substantially shocked by the event. I don't think he ever joined me on a fishing trip again, though he and his family did consume the results of many of my subsequent fishing trips. I myself was under no illusion whatsoever as to how close a brush this had been with Mother Ocean.

Above: *The biggest 'cracker from the George era, weighing 32 lb, caught in November 1974, on crab, from Kabeljoubank near Victoria Bay.*

I caught some beautiful big fish while living in George, but was unhappy with my work situation and wished to fulfil a dream of working in aquaculture. One day an advertisement appeared in one of the major newspapers seeking someone to work on black mussel culture research with the Fisheries Development Corporation of South Africa. Where?

"Bloody heck – *Saldanha*! Sheeesh man, I've just

come from that fishless doldrum. Why can't it be in Mozambique? The fishing's brilliant there."

However, I wanted to get into aquaculture and positions were not plentiful – it was an industry in its infancy. Furthermore, I had no qualifications and knew that degrees were the key to this door unless one was very, very lucky. I decided to ask Professor Margaret M Smith of the famed J.L.B. Smith Institute of Ichthyology in Grahamstown for help in the form of a personal reference. Fortunately I was in a position to do so.

As a child I idolised Prof. JLB Smith, the scientist famous for identifying the coelacanth (*Latimeria chalumnae*). He was an incredible inspiration to me. Unfortunately, he died before I could meet him. However his much younger wife, Prof. Margaret M Smith, took over from him as director of the institute and I had been able to send her many specimens taken from the depths by Sea Harvest's trawlers while I worked there. This amazing woman seemed tireless in her efforts, and I still have many wonderful letters of encouragement from her, with thanks for my contributions.

Only in her later years when sadly she was confined to a wheel-chair, was I lucky enough to meet her. I was delivering some freshwater aquarium fish (with which I was farming in Zululand at the time) to the institute for its collection. I decided to show them to her first.

"Pooooh!" she said. "What are those things? They aren't SEA fish!"

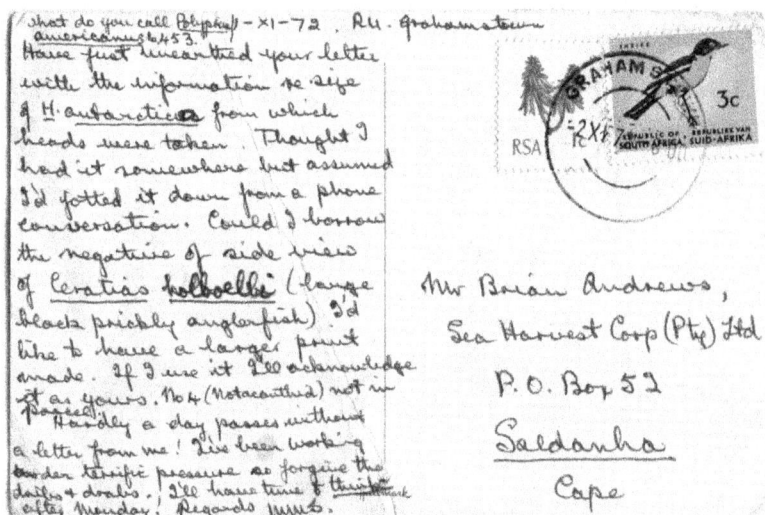

Above: *A typical handwritten communication from Prof. MM Smith.*

There weren't too many fish around that Prof. Smith didn't recognise; I think she was just a little scornful of foreign species, especially freshwater ones, which these fish certainly were.

When she received my polite request for a reference, she provided, very promptly and with her usual wonderful grace, a letter which I could just about have used to apply for the position of prime minister. I remain enormously grateful. There is no question that she secured my launch into aquaculture. I got the job and headed back to Saldanha, my BMW tied onto the back of a Ford Cortina bakkie (ute) along with the rest of my worldly possessions.

My second sojourn to Saldanha was happily short-lived. Two months after I arrived there the black mussel research project was shelved and I was sent to Zululand.

Chapter 5

Zululand. Estuary and Sea Fishing: A Fascinating Variety of Fish (Plus Pranks, Broken Rods and an Airborne Vehicle)

The director of the Fisheries Development Corporation of South Africa called me into his office in Cape Town. I stood at his massive desk wondering what this was all about. I'd only been with the FDC for two months. I would soon find out. With Mr du Plessis, one never had to wait long to be presented with the meat of the matter at hand.

"Brian, as you know, our black mussel project is to be discontinued. How would you like to work on prawns in Zululand?"

My brain rattled, registered and my mind screamed "*Zululand*? WHOA MAN! Would I like to move from Saldanha to ZULULAND? Bloody hell, YOU BETCHA!" My mouth, more sensibly, but not without feeling, said, "I'd absolutely love to!"

"Good. How soon can you leave?" he asked with a slightly raised eyebrow. If I'd said I needed a week I would have expected him to say, "Can you make it sooner?" So I said, "Tomorrow if necessary."

"Excellent my boy, that's what I like to hear. You'll spend a month or two in Knysna learning how to culture algae, then go to Zululand. Good luck."

Out I went walking on air, knowing there would be no small talk following. I couldn't believe my good fortune – a couple of months in the beautiful town of Knysna and then on to Zululand.

I most certainly fished while in Knysna, but have no recollections or photos of catches. Thereafter I loaded the BMW bike onto the back of my Cortina bakkie and off I went as fast as its 1600 cc engine could carry me. Passing through Grahamstown on my way north I stopped and visited an old friend, Martin Davies, at the JLB Smith Institute of Ichthyology where he was doing research work on eel culture. 'Fartin Martin' I called him, because of the way the name rolled so smoothly off the tongue, not because of any predisposition to bowel bloating on his part – that was *my* speciality. He suggested that we take a fishing trip to the Cowie River at Port Alfred while I was available.

"Absolutely impossible, unless you insist!" I said. He was excellent company and good fun to fish with and I didn't know when we'd meet again.

We didn't catch much but the absence of fish was compensated for by loads of belly laughs between bouts of extreme irritation. Initially the irritation was his and the laughter mine, but unfortunately such an excellent scenario was too good to last.

We fished the bank of the river for some hours, my expectation riding high on his promises of excellent fishing. My expectations dropped from high, to realistic, to acknowledging a familiar scenario – the place was dead. Time to punish Mr Davies for falsely raising my hopes.

I sneaked up next to him, capturing his attention by pointing to a fictitious bird or something up river. *This* fishing was better; he took the bait, hook, line and sinker. As he peered into the distance straining to see what wasn't there, I carefully put my hand on the lower part of the fishing rod he was holding. He was no longer really waiting in expectation of a bite, except for his subconscious – which never loses hope – and noticed nothing. I pushed down firmly on his rod.

"SHII-IITT!" he bellowed and struck with such force as to unseat himself from the rock on which he was perched. I nearly vomited with laughter.

Of course he realized immediately what had happened and cursed me accordingly, threatening retaliation. Incredibly, over the next hour or two I was able to repeat this performance several times on a trusting Martin, who while his trust seemed limitless, made up for this with increasing irritation, cursing and threats, while my own laughter grew proportionately more raucous.

Had I continued in this vein I might well have split a bodily seam, but suddenly and surprisingly, I caught a little fish which could be used as a live-bait. I wasn't going to miss the opportunity and rigged for it with great urgency. Out it went, my attention focussed once again on more important matters.

The incoming tide slowed and changed direction. We fished and peace reigned. Martin, in typical tolerant fashion, showed no vengeful signs. I waited patiently.

Live-baits can be slow but tend to deliver good fish. Suddenly my line tightened. I was holding the rod, and immediately released the spool fully, allowing the line to run freely but preventing an over-run by thumbing it lightly. I looked over at Martin who was sitting there looking interested – fascinated in fact.

"Something running here," I said in brusque businesslike fashion, with just a hint of, "you've got to use a decent bait if you want to fish seriously." Martin was using pillie or something inferior like that. He said nothing. I returned my attention to my line which had stopped running.

"Damn, it's stopped," I muttered with concern. As I spoke the fish took off again. I allowed it a brief moment and struck forcefully. Again, hard, and again. I was on, and the fish took line against my drag.

"Good looking fish!" I shouted, though Martin was only five or six metres from me.

He was now bent over with concentrated interest, his rod still in hand. I wondered vaguely why intense interest should bring about such a twisting of his body. Still, there was a fish to beat and I focussed on that. All of a sudden I felt that horrible juddering of my line going over the rocks. I lightened the pressure, cursed, and tried flicking the rod at various different angles to free the line. Martin smiled at me. He was obviously acknowledging my superior skills and wishing me luck. In desperation at not being able to free my line, the fish all the while making its presence known, I took off my shoes and socks and made a stumbling entry into the water at its rocky edge. As I slid and fell about the slippery rocks I made an increasingly concerted effort to free the fish, ending up soaked – and unsuccessful.

Eventually Martin could contain himself no longer. He tried, but the strain was too great. His laughter burst through his nose in a magnitude of snort that is likely to produce an unwanted jet of nasal mucus. The bastard! No wonder he was bent over and twisted in concentration. He was hiding the fact that he had hooked my line as the tide carried it past him. Cunning blighter, he had made like a fish, pulling my line slowly, jerking it, and letting a little out from time to time. He laughed till the tears flowed – for a long time, long after I told him it was enough. What a warped sense of humour some people have!

Never mind, something he gave me to eat for lunch enabled me to punish his olfactory senses for the entire drive home; worthwhile even if it meant living with stomach gripes and his window fully open for the cold night drive. Funny that *his* stomach wasn't affected...

I said goodbye to Martin and Grahamstown and headed north towards Zululand with an uplifted heart. Zululand – home of the mighty kingfish (giant trevally, *Caranx ignobilis* to Australians). I didn't know it then, but I would have to wait for Australia to realize my kingfish/trevally dreams. Soon after arrival, I found myself based on the well known Amatikulu estuary about a hundred kilometres north of Durban, on the banks of which the Fisheries Development Corporation's prawn research unit was situated. Fishing from the shores of an estuary or river is for some reason generally *far* less productive than fishing from a boat, so I temporarily suspended my anti boat-fishing rules. Not that I had anything remotely resembling a marlin boat.

What I did have access to was a beautiful wide canoe called *'Dabulamanzi'* (meaning 'Cleaver of the water' in Zulu) which some kind friends lent to me, and in which I was not infrequently towed along for considerable distances by large aquatic animals. Secondly, I had the use of an ancient wooden boat propelled by a slightly less ancient 15 hp Suzuki outboard motor. The outboard was very reliable but the boat leaked in a most puzzling fashion. That is to say it had a mind of its own – it sometimes leaked and it sometimes didn't. I was never able to fathom what made it decide whether to leak or not. It was safer always to carry bailing equipment. Nor could I find a particular place in the boat at which a leak occurred. I think it was more of an osmotic situation in which water moved through a sometimes permeable barrier from a high density of water to a slightly lower one.

In all honesty, what was even more puzzling was why it didn't just sink. Its plywood structure had seen better days, and I had to be very careful not to put heavy equipment or even a body part through it. I have one photograph of the canoe, and none of the wooden boat. No one in their right mind would have photographed that. Having said that, I have to admit that it carried me through many a dark night to some very good fish.

One of those good fish comes immediately to mind, but before getting to that, a description of a typical night's fishing on 'the boat' will help the reader to have a clearer picture of the situation. The boat was nameless. I called it a few things from time to time, but refrained from painting any of these names on the hull – the owner might have objected.

Many of the trips were overnight excursions – I exhibited considerable, often grim, determination in my younger days. Trips generally started off with a planning phase after the decision to go out had been made. This planning phase usually commenced half way through the workday, most commonly but not always, on a Friday. The rest of the day was dedicated to organising and preparing.

Most usefully, prawn farm work, especially research, included many activities closely related to fishing.

"Just checking the motor before I go for some mullet; need some to feed the prawn broodstock. I'll do the boat at the same time; needs bailing apart from anything else."

Thoughts of fishing dominated work-related thoughts to the latter's absolute exclusion. I justified my lack of contribution to the afternoon's work (albeit only to myself) by pointing out how responsible I was in fact being. Working with the prawns when my attention was on fishing would have been downright irresponsible and could have caused a serious mishap. If nothing else, I was at least a responsible employee.

Immediately after work, everything already having been prepared, I grabbed some prawns and pillies for bait, my fishing gear, and a very few items of clothing. (Won't be cold tonight...) I wasn't married then so there was no need to invest time in family matters such as goodbyes, which might have taken such form as:

"I'm heading off now, you don't mind do you dear? Bye now, I'll see you tomorrow...You DO mind? But...but..."

The fact that I was unmarried probably saved an average of thirty minutes of precious fishing time per trip. If possible I would leave in the daylight as I had no sophisticated equipment such as echo sounders to help locate the desired spots. Instead, I got to know the estuary's deep and shallow parts by a mixture of 'echo sounding' with an inverted fishing rod, or running aground, which eventually enabled me to find my way around comfortably using visual landmarks and intuition.

If possible I would acquire some live mullet with a cast net before leaving, if this had not already been accomplished on a 'broodstock food' collecting trip.

Upon reaching the most promising looking spot – a decision as always entailing enormous procrastination - the depth would be confirmed by the anchor on its rope, and baits would be prepared and cast without delay. Late in the afternoon in summer the action could be very brisk, especially at the turn of a high tide. At best, the number of lines which could be handled by one person would drop to not more than one, only to creep back up to three or even four as the action quietened down.

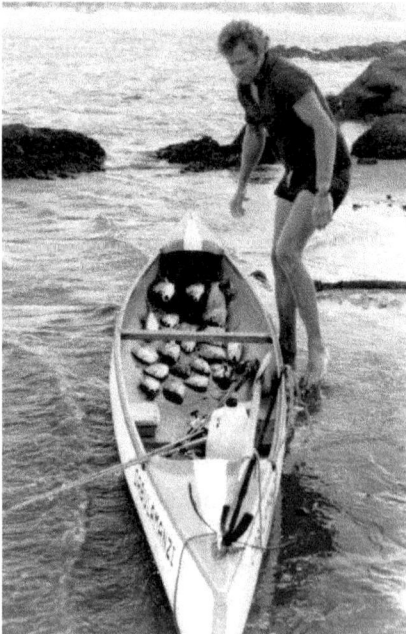

Left: *The canoe 'Dabulamanzi' with an example of Amatikulu estuary's amazing variety of fish species.*

The variety of species encountered in this estuary never ceased to amaze me. It is too extensive to list in full here, but included spotted, silver and cock grunter, (*Pomadasys operculare, P. multimaculatus,* and *P. hasta* resp.) shad (tailor), kob (mulloway), skipjack (giant herring), rock salmon (mangrove jack), small kingfish (trevally) and barracuda, rock cod, bream and stumpnose, as well as mud crabs and of course the inevitable sharks and rays.

A north easterly breeze seemed to be conducive to strong feeding activity and the choppy surface also made the fish less shy. It would be rare for there to be no action at all as the late afternoon light faded slowly into darkness. Night time was quieter but tended to yield bigger fish, and that was what called me with the loudest voice. An hour or two into darkness could be good, as could an hour or two before midnight. Around midnight it tended to be dead, and thereafter till daybreak was very slow, with the exception of big kob (mulloway) for which the chances of capture were then at their best. Rays and sharks could be encountered anytime, and mud crabs, with their bait-destroying habits, could be a pest for parts of the night.

After arrival I would normally fish hard for the first few hours, then as things quietened, a more relaxed approach could be adopted with fast acting prawns or pilchard being replaced by a slower live-bait or two. Relaxed? Well, relaxed for as long as a leaking boat would allow. After midnight not even fishing could fight off the body's natural inclination to doze off. Due to the boat's leak, falling asleep could be a problem, and as staying awake in the early hours of the morning could be extremely difficult, equipment had to be stowed well above the floorboards to avoid inundation by sea water during long non-bailing periods. Inundation was good for the fishy smell but was very bad for some items of tackle and spare clothes. Mind you, the dew would wet them almost as thoroughly, though at least that was not salty.

Such a night out would normally entail eventually curling up as comfortably as possible (or should I say as *least un*comfortably as possible) on the narrow bench seats, when fishing action was at its lowest ebb and therefore staying awake was most difficult. It was also from this time onwards that the dew would settle its insidious cloak of moisture over everything, especially on my less than adequately covered body.

Waking up periodically and finding the enthusiasm to sit up, rub the eyes, stretch, reel in, check and re-bait hooks took considerable will power. Sometimes such will power simply wasn't available and it took a scary bilge water level to stir me to bailing action. Then, having thus warmed myself up, I would have woken up sufficiently to attend to the hooks. I usually had three or four lines out at once. It made sense that if one were going to torture oneself to this degree, then the odds of catching something might as well be raised as high as possible. Usually a heavier hand-line baited with a live mullet would be added to the three-rod team. This would go straight to the bottom in the hope of attracting the attention of a passing rock salmon (*Lutjanus argentimaculatus*), the same species as the Australian mangrove jack.

Left: *6 lb rock salmon and 5 lb cock grunter.*

Needless to say, tangles occurred from time to time despite my best efforts to either retrieve the remaining lines while playing a fish or to manoeuvre the fish around or between them. With neither option being easily executed, some totally irreversible tangles occurred in the dark.

Rock salmon were the welcome wakers of the early morning shift. The ratchet scream of a hand-line being stripped from a rod-less reel, secured to the boat to prevent it from taking off into the water, would have the guaranteed effect of waking me instantly. The rock salmons' sudden vigorous attacks on a bait, though infrequent, were unambiguous, and hooking them was happily almost a foregone conclusion.

Right: *4 lb kob, 7 lb rock cod, and 7 & 6 lb 'alarm clock' rock salmon.*

An energetic fight, terminating in netting or gaffing one of them, would transform an unsuccessful night into a successful one. These beautiful looking, hard fighting, highly palatable estuary dwellers, sometimes weighing as much as six or seven pounds, made a fine prize. I wouldn't be at all surprised if these fish on occasion, with their alarm-clock strikes, saved me from drowning or at least from losing the boat and motor, by waking me in time to prevent capsizing or sinking as the boat took on water. How did I repay them? By putting them on the braai (barbeque) of course! We humans are a shameless lot.

The trip I am about to recount was typical of the early years before that beautiful, wild estuary became so silted up that one could virtually walk across it in places. The mouth was at the southern end at the time. This is significant because its mouth would creep progressively northwards through the sand, or close up altogether until it was blasted out by a violent Zululand flood, far south of its pre-flood position. Big fish, in fact fish in general, seemed more plentiful when the mouth was situated to the south.

On this occasion I boarded the boat equipped for a dark moonless night. At the time the boat's leak rate was moderate to bad, which meant bailing preferably at least once every hour or so. Up until about 1.00 am the night was normal in terms of discomfort levels and lower than usual in terms of catches. All live-bait had been used up. I had dozed off and was too lethargic to admit defeat and go home. At my last period of useful wakefulness I had bailed the bottom of the boat to near empty, and baited up two 12 lb lines each with a cluster of bait prawns on a 2/0 hook. (I used mainly Kencors and an Ambassador reel on light estuary rods of unrecalled make.) This done and lines cast out, I then dozed off again, knowing that my bait was likely to be stolen by some unknown thief, and that if anything half decent was going to have a chance at it, it would have to hurry itself.

I was, most happily, dead wrong. Nothing touched at least one of the baits for an hour or so, leaving it tastily intact to be found eventually by a food seeker of considerable proportions. That maw could have engulfed dozens of baits of that size all at once, but evidently there wasn't much else on the menu, so the trifling titbit was deemed acceptable. The first I knew of the decision to dine was the usual scream of a ratchet. No stiff creaking body or dull blinking eyes under these circumstances – all were bypassed in a dive for the rod and a hard strike. SHITE! Whatever had nailed the bait seemed to have the dimensions of a small submarine. I must have hooked its tonsils and annoyed it for its response was to take off in the opposite direction at an impressive rate of knots, hard drag notwithstanding.

Surprisingly, it chose to swim *against* a strong tidal flow on this impressive first run. Had it swum *with* the flow, I may well not have been able to turn it before running out of line, which it would have snapped with ease. As it was, the fish was fighting tide *and* drag, a not inconsiderable task even for a large fish. For this reason alone I was able, eventually, to turn the fish – not back towards me, but even better, in a sideways movement. It moved fairly slowly in a wide arc from the starboard side of the boat to the port side, a fairly long distance considering that it had taken what I estimated to be at least 60 metres of line. Inexplicably, it continued to stay far ahead of the anchored boat and fight the current at the same time.

I did nothing to discourage this strategy, and was surprised but very pleased when it turned and repeated the same arc in the opposite direction. In this sense the fight could not have gone better for me. I still didn't know what it was, but it wasn't fighting like a shark or ray. Eventually I felt the occasional head 'knock' which spelled the likelihood of an edible fish, probably a kob, considering its size. The fight took on a new meaning. An unknown species had to be taken seriously until its identity was known. By my reckoning a shark or ray, once known, was neither here nor there, and in prime fishing time could be an annoying waste of time and bait. But a strongly suspected large edible fish immediately produced an approach of cautious strategy and great care.

I reduced the drag slightly to minimize the chances of a broken knot, snapped line or broken hook in the event of a strong lunge. Then I started trying to retrieve line carefully. Always better to have as much line as possible available in case the fish took off with the current. Had it done so, I would certainly have done what I had done many times in the past in both the boat and canoe: up-anchor. The canoe was light enough to be towed along, but in the boat the outboard had to be started and used to regain line, usually with considerable difficulty because it had to be done in reverse and single-handed, after lifting the anchor, while still holding onto the rod. Fortunately, when it came to lifting the anchor, the estuary was rarely more than three metres deep.

But this fish consistently maintained a head-into-the-current stance while I pulled it slowly backwards towards the boat, being extremely careful to make my movements very smooth and jerk-free so as to avoid startling it into a panic move. While I was playing the fish, I switched on my headlamp and beamed its light in the direction of my line. "Crikey, still miles away!" It had taken a great deal of line and I just had to be patient. My slow careful retrieve continued until the fish was almost in line with the boat, still facing upstream, but still quite a few metres away and out of sight, though now quite close to the surface. I had progressively reduced the drag and pressure that I was putting on it. I was winning and there was no hurry. Amazingly that old enemy the anchor rope had, at least up till now, been no danger at all. My every move was taut with anxiety. So many big fish are lost at the last minute.

Suddenly the fish materialized in the torch's beam and my heart missed a beat. It was a whacking great kob (jewfish), just idling along at the end of my line, right on the surface as though nothing was amiss. I knew *that* would change at some point before I got the fish on board, like when it detected the boat or the gaff detected it. I continued the low pressure to bring it alongside. It was obviously tired, but against 12 lb line and a light rod it would still pack a potentially hazardous punch, no doubt about that. With one hand I reached for my short boat gaff – hardly a match for this fellow, but it was all I had. I would not be putting my hand inside *those* gills until it was well and truly beaten. I waited until it was within striking distance and struck with the gaff.

The gaff hooked solid and the fish woke up instantly. In a single powerful stroke it drenched me, contemptuously shook itself free of the gaff, and took off under the boat, threatening to negate all of the good fortune the battle had delivered so far. Up towards the anchor rope went the line.

"Oh shit no, please don't let this happen!" (Familiar words?)

Then I felt the friction of my line stretching and scraping around the anchor rope in that horrible juddering way that it does. "Oh *NO-OO!*"

The line pulled jerkily off the reel as I waited for the worst. Then incredibly, no more juddering. Miraculously it had moved free of the rope, a rare, *rare* outcome. I sweated in the cool of the night as the line moved steadily away from the hazard.

The whole process of slow retrieval recommenced. This time when it surfaced within reach the fish was sufficiently exhausted to be unable to break away from the gaff, but not too tired to drench me thoroughly again with mighty strokes of its tail. With one hand very carefully positioned under a gill away from the gill rakers and with the gaff solidly placed, I hoisted the fish on board, taking care to lower it gently to avoid having it go through the bottom of the boat. Thankfully it didn't thrash around in the water in there – it was beaten.

Forty pounds of beautiful kob lay in the boat.

Interestingly, within the same week I landed another kob, 30 lbs this time, in the same area. The fight was shorter but more varied and vigorous, and I ended up beaching the boat and continuing the final stages of the fight from the bank, making the end game far easier.

Right: *30 lb kob,
Amatikulu estuary,
1978*

Left: *40 lb kob caught
on prawn, Amatikulu
estuary, 1978.*

The estuary delivered many fish and more than a few surprises. It was here that I unwittingly threw a cast net over a shark which I estimated to be about 100 cm in length. The water was dirty and quite shallow. I was throwing the net for mullet. Not surprisingly, when the shark found itself suddenly surrounded by nylon netting, it made an immediate bid for freedom. The net erupted in a thrashing of water in all directions. The shark's grey body appeared briefly and I was able to identify it before, fortunately for the net, it found its way out underneath. I don't know who was more surprised, the shark or myself – perhaps it was equal. I would love to know what it told its friends when it eventually slowed down enough to speak. Amazingly there was not a mark on the net.

On another occasion I was called when one of the research unit's Zulu employees, Sipho, was stung by a lionfish (*Pterois volitans*), a very painful experience. It is the only occasion on which I have seen a pale Zulu, with beads of perspiration clearly visible against the pallor. He was stoically silent but obviously unhappy, his hand noticeably swollen. I immediately heated some water to considerably hotter than bearable, then carefully reduced it to just bearable, and got him to slowly immerse his hand in it. He did so, maintaining stoic silence in true Zulu tradition. I swear I saw his hair straighten a little, while the pallor took on a pink hue, and the beads of perspiration doubled in size and number. After a remarkably short time he relaxed visibly, his teeth appeared in a smile, and their contrast with his complexion returned to normal as the pallor subsided. I was most impressed, having read of this treatment for various marine stings but never having been able to test its efficacy. Thank you, Sipho, for the opportunity.

A further unusual event involved a Zulu employee called Zablon which occurred while he was netting with a drag-net for mullet to feed the prawn broodstock. He emerged from the water after freeing the net from some obstacle, with a large mud crab (*Scylla serrata*) attached to the middle of his back. I did not witness this while the crab was still attached, but saw the marks. The offending crab was beaten off with a stick. It would have taken some beating – I hope the blows were well aimed. Life was never dull for long around the estuary.

In this Zululand period I was also fortunate enough to visit and fish the beautiful Mapelane and Cape Vidal areas, but did not get as far as Kosi Bay, which in South African waters is the home of enormous kingfish (*Caranx ignobilis*, giant trevally in Australia), though they are occasionally encountered further south. I experienced two losses of big fish further south which were both very likely the much wanted kingfish. The first was hooked on a live shad. In this case, during a powerful fight on heavy tackle, which included a *lot* of line being stripped, the single hook pulled out. The strength and style of fight and the fact that the nylon trace was not bitten off left me reasonably convinced it was a kingfish.

The second fish, judging by its dogged fight and end tactics, and the fact that it took a tin spoon (lure), was almost certainly a kingfish. It took the spoon off the ledges south of the beach entrance at Cape Vidal late one afternoon. After a strong unrelenting fight so characteristic of the species, during which I had managed with great difficulty to hold it away from various patches of reef, it tired sufficiently for me to persuade it to approach an area of beach where just a few outcrops of rock stood between myself and victory.

But even one rock is sufficient for any self respecting kingfish, and so to my intense horror, it made for one of these and lodged itself behind it. I immediately waded into the warm clear water, bracing myself repeatedly against breaking waves to get as near to the offending sandstone outcrop as I possibly could. But try as I might, and that was plenty, the fish wouldn't budge. Eventually the line parted and the much desired kingfish was lost. After all that. So close, so very, very close!

There were another two interesting fishing-related events at Cape Vidal in which fish played only a fairly minor role. I was in my Mazda bakkie (ute in Australian parlance) and had driven several kilometres up the beach to do a spot of night fishing off some flat ledges at low tide. Although the Mazdas were only 2WD, with wide and sufficiently deflated tyres they were remarkably good even on deep soft sand, though speed was needed to negotiate particularly bad patches and access-ramps.

The sea was in a kind mood and soon I had a kob or two of around eight to ten pounds in the bag, caught on pillie. I hooked another, a little larger, which threw the hook just after I had lifted it onto the ledge. I had used a small wave to help with the lifting, and the retreating water now threatened to take the fish home to its mother.

No way was I letting that happen. I dropped my rod and reel on the ledge, and grabbed for the fish, headlamp probing the shallow, frothy water. The fish was swimming as hard as it could but was semi stranded in the shallows, giving me the opportunity to grasp it and get a hand under a gill plate. It thrashed about, and as it did so, another wave came over the ledge and my quarry broke free once more. In the dark that was the last I saw of it.

My hand was bleeding profusely, having been cut quite extensively by the gill rakers. Annoyed, I looked around for my rod and reel. The large rod was a favourite which I had purchased second-hand some years before from the George café owner of bad betting repute. No sign of it. The water had run off the ledge (of course, now that the fish was gone) and the beam of my headlamp was put to work: up/down, left/right, near and far. No sign of it. It had been washed 'overboard' while I was busy losing my fish. Double damn and shit!

After a few more minutes of fruitless searching I ungraciously admitted defeat and left the ledge. I cleaned the less fortunate fishes, and prepared to leave. As I was about to drive off I decided to give the rocks one more scan, just in case…

Instead of confining the search to the immediate area, I walked northwards along the ledge, sweeping the lamp left and right, and beaming it occasionally into the distance.

Then, out of the blackness, an object appeared which looked far more like fishing tackle than rock formation. WHA-HOA! It was my rod and reel, a good hundred metres away from where I had lost it. I couldn't believe my good fortune. The reel was jammed with sand which told me the outfit must have been washed off the ledge by the backwash, rolled over a sandy bottom, then been spewed back out again. Incredible! I was amazed and delighted.

I secured the rod with its two mates (which I'm sure were equally delighted to see it) sticking out of the back of the ute under the canopy's door, and drove off along the beach while the tide was still low enough to do so. Up the ramp and into the camp ground I drove, swung the vehicle round, threw it into reverse and manoeuvred back under a tree.

"CUURR-R*AACCKK*!"

"OHH, SHITSAKES, what the FFFF*UUU*CK was that?"

The question was a subconscious response; the me on the surface knew exactly what '*that*' was. '*That*' was my rods losing an argument with the tree.

Of the three rods, two, including my old friend which had just suffered a near-death-experience in the sea, were suffering what a rod doctor would have described as terminal fractures. *They* may not have been bleeding, but I sure as hell was. My own description of their state would have employed a less medical term – a familiar one, in the past tense. I was devastated. Amazingly the Silaflex rod

had remained intact despite being subjected to the same extreme forces, tough old devil that it was.

On the matter of my spontaneous verbal outburst in response to the cracking sound in which a couple of well known four letter words were employed, upon being told this story by an acquaintance, a particular listener expressed surprise:

"I didn't know that Brian uses *that* sort of language!" he exclaimed.

Well, if he has doubts and wants verification via direct experience, he has only to be present when I break a rod, lose a fish, get a hook in my hand, etc. The opportunities are endless. There is absolutely no need to remain deprived.

Before leaving Cape Vidal and its mixed bag of events, let me tell a story of 'half the fun is getting there'...if one likes drama, that is. I was once again

travelling up the beach, this time as fast as possible. I had a
fair way to go and was concerned with running out of 'low-
tide-bitumen'. I know the photo shows a lot of sand, but I
am extremely cautious in such matters. (Like money,
bakkies do not grow on trees.) All of a sudden the 'road'
rose up to meet me and I experienced what fighter jet pilots
must experience when taking off from a sloped launching
ramp on an aircraft carrier – except that they expect it…

ZOOOOOM---WHUNK!!!...OOOPS!

"*OOHOOMPH!*" I blurted out as I hit the natural
sandy ramp and my stomach embraced my oesophagus. I
was instantly airborne. Moments later I landed with an
almighty WHUNK. The bakkie dug in and came to a
sudden halt which produced a hard bonk of chin on the
steering wheel. Again I "OOMPHED" as my inner parts
contorted for a second time.

"My GOD! What have I done?"

Above: *Airborne! The trackless flight path
viewed from the launch side. (Note the un-
tyre-marked section with investigatory
footprints.)*

After confirming that my vertebrae were still
functioning independently, I worked up the courage to look
out of the side window. I expected to see a tyre staring at
me through it. I expected *all* the wheels to be staring at me
from modified alignments. But no, all was in order thanks
to Mazda, and substantially deflated tyres. I paced out six
metres between take-off and landing. The flight's height
was unknown but considerable, judging by the whunk on
landing. I slowed down after that; after all as I said,
bakkies don't grow on trees.

Above: *The 'Flying Mazda' posing on a better day with the author, and a yellowtail and kob, caught on another occasion on the beautiful Wild Coast.*

Chapter 6
The Transkei Wild Coast! Amazing Catches, Big Fish Landed...and Lost, Two Fifty-Three Pounders, a Nose-Picking Diversion, and My Biggest Fish To Date

I first visited Port St Johns and Coffee Bay on the Transkei's Wild Coast with my parents during school holidays. I loved it from day one. I have two particularly clear memories of Port St Johns, the first of which relates to the capture of my first kob at the age of nine or ten years. This story ended abruptly when the fish, of between one and two pounds, fell into a deep crack in the rocks, and stayed there. It stayed there despite Herculean efforts on my part to extract it. That could quite well be one of the reasons why I have directed my efforts at bigger fish ever since. They don't disappear into cracks in rocks quite so easily.

For example, had the fish been the same size as those in the second story about Port St Johns, the loss would not have occurred. My family was holidaying there and one afternoon we were all throwing tin spoons (lures) in the Umzimvubu River mouth in the hope of persuading a big kob to eat metal. The kob runs were legendary in those days, and as luck would have it my mother and father each hooked a big fish. After gargantuan battles the fish were both landed, the watching crowd raising a congratulatory cheer as my mother's fish was beached after an hour, on fairly light tackle.

Both fish were large and apparently reasonably similar in weight, but one was distinctly longer and thinner while the other was noticeably shorter and fatter. Naturally friendly disagreement broke out over whose fish was bigger. This went on for a while until it was realized that valuable fishing time was being wasted. The debate was put on hold. Spoons were sent to hunt kob and the matter was put to sleep for the moment, especially when my father hooked another big fish. This specimen fought like an absolute Trojan and everyone thought it would knock the socks off the other two. The scrap went on for ages, and it was only when the great body approached that it could be seen why. It had been foul-hooked in the tail and was in fact smaller than the other two.

Right: *My parents with my mother's 53 lb kob of family dispute fame. The mouth of the magnificent Umzimvubu River is in the background. Amazing that such a placid piece of water could be harbouring so many big fish.*

Of course this rekindled the earlier argument over the size of the first two fish, and amidst heated discussion we made our way to the local hotel which offered the services of its large scale to arbitrate in such fishy disputes. The first fish settled on exactly 53 lb, give or take zero. Down it came and up went the second fish. Silence reigned as the scale stopped its bouncing and the needle settled – on exactly 53 lb, give or take zero. No amount of will power or changing the angle at which one viewed the scale's needle could change the facts. The dispute was thus fairly resolved. The foul-hooked fish weighed 40 lb.

The story doesn't quite end there. My parents donated the fish to the Ugie Orphanage, which used to take its charges on an annual holiday from the Eastern Cape to Port

St Johns. The following year my parents visited again, and chanced to be at a local market just when a large goose was being auctioned. They bid on the goose but eventually regretfully missed out. Some time later, still at the market, they bumped into and recognised the same gentleman from the Ugie Orphanage to whom they had given the fish the previous year. Upon recognising them, this gent immediately offered – and insisted they take – a large goose he had just successfully bid on at an auction. Yep, one and the same, proving yet again that it's a small world and that what goes around comes around.

My appetite for the Wild Coast was thus whetted at a young age, but it was not until many years later that it was able to deliver the goods.

In 1976, in the earlier part of my Zululand stay, I had the good fortune to meet Tony Simpson, a very accomplished angler who specialised in the same type of fish as I aspired to myself – big ones! Tony, who lived in Eshowe, KwaZulu-Natal, did me one of the greatest favours anyone has ever done me; he introduced me to Mbolompo Point on the Transkei coast.

Tony is a veteran of Mbolompo and surrounds; long before I first met him he had caught enough big fish there to make me green with envy. At the time of writing he continues to fish the place, and continues to produce tales that turn me green. This magnificent area just south of Hole in the Wall provided me with the most superb fishing I have done anywhere in South Africa. Very isolated and quite difficult to get to in those days, and even more difficult to get out of, we generally had the place to ourselves, though we did have to help a very misguided caravanner out on one occasion.

Mbolompo is onomatopoeically named after the deep rumbling sound made by the rock-melon sized round boulders that roll up and down a narrow but deep gully near the point. As waves roar into the entrance, these boulders roll up the gully, and as the water subsides, they roll down again, producing the unmistakable sound of Mbolompo. Table Rock, a magnificent fishing spot at Mbolompo Point, is situated about 30 minutes walk away from where we usually camped at Lubanzi beach, or 15 minutes walk from another camp which was reached via some very steep up or downhill bits. It was uphill going back, which of course was the fish-carrying haul. Almost without exception we fished Table Rock twice daily: morning and evening. With big fish to carry, it was a fair hike, especially in the dark.

Left: *Carrying the evening's catch of kob home.*

On my first trip to the area we camped at Lubanzi, the beautiful stretch of beach north of the point. Tony not only took his fishing seriously; he took his camping and camp food seriously too. I know about the food because we had bets on the biggest fish caught every day, and the loser had to prepare all of the following day's meals. Preparing an egg to satisfy Tony's fastidious taste was more challenging than trying not to lose the bet in the first place. As a bachelor, when I first met Tony, my cooking skills extended only as far as rendering the food no longer technically raw. He was insistent, and helped not only my catches, but my cooking skills as well.

On the very first evening of this first trip I had the good fortune to land my first yellowtail (*Seriola lalandi* – kingfish to those from downunder) of 29 lb, on a pillie. Early next morning I landed a 19 lb poensie. What an introduction to this paradise! Such luck couldn't last – and didn't.

Right: *29 lb yellowtail and 19 lb poensie on the first Mbolompo trip, 1976.*

Very early on the second last morning I hoisted out an almost too-large live shad for bait. Fortunately the water was deep immediately in front of Table Rock, so I got away with a cast of just a few metres which was all I could manage with a bait weighing close to 2 lb.

The line dropped almost vertically, uncomfortably near to the rocks. Eventually, I felt rocky contact with the line somewhere beneath the surface – not something one wants with a live-bait of any kind. I tried to work the line free but was unable to do so, and decided to leave it be, sit back, and soak in the sun's first rays. I had no more live-baits anyway. Some minutes later I felt the line stir and start to pull. Incredibly it was free of the rocks. I gave the fish the usual period of time to swallow, hit as hard as I could four or five times and then maintained a heavy pumping action, also as hard as I could.

Anything that could swallow a bait that size was going to be big trouble. The fish made immediately for an underwater reef to the right, just as Tony had warned me the area's big poensies were inclined to do. Preventing them from reaching it was critical if they were to be landed. Even with 60 lb line this could sometimes prove impossible, and I was having one hell of a battle making it possible on this occasion.

Eventually, to my enormous relief, the monster turned and swung left. From then on the fight remained relatively close, with line being lost and retrieved, lost and retrieved. It was like fighting a slowly moving large tree trunk except for occasional lunges and head jerks, distinctly edible-feeling. Mbolompo generally delivered a surprisingly high proportion of 'edible' fish relative to sharks and rays. After around twenty minutes the fish began to tire and my thoughts became more focussed on landing it. The best option was to lead it if possible past where I was standing, to the left and into the deep sheltered gully situated there. Once there, unless it managed to rebuild a head of steam, it was as close to being in the bag as a fish on the end of a line can be. There is a marvellously safe, protected gaffing ledge there.

For some unfortunate reason, instead of staying and fighting from Table Rock, as Tony had recommended earlier, as the tide was low I jumped down onto an exposed rock closer to the sea. Seconds after I had done so a swell came past me from right to left. This wasn't just *any* swell. This was the swell sent to deliver the fish into my hands. As it swept past it carried the fish towards the safe haven of the gaffing gully. But instead of being delighted, as I certainly should have been, I was horrified – I was in the wrong position to take advantage. Instead of moving freely round the corner to victory, the line tightened around a rock as the fish was swept along, still deep and unseen.

I was using a Tattler No. IV, a large, rugged reel loaded with 60 lb line. At that critical moment I had a choice: decrease the drag or free the spool totally. Whichever I chose I had to do instantly – a speedy decision which only a brain under pressure can make quickly enough. Unfortunately mine made the wrong one. I chose to free the spool totally, by pulling back the lever. On the

Tattler, with the line under pressure the lever will not release freely. While I didn't know it at the time, I certainly do now.

The line tightened round the rock as I sweated with the lever, frantically trying to force it back towards me. *CRACK!* The line parted like a pistol shot moments before victory should have been mine. I teetered backwards, recovered my balance, and stood in a state of stunned shock and disbelief. Never before had I come so close to hurling my rod and reel into the sea. It was an overwhelming impulse and it took me some moments to regain what was left of my composure and overcome the feelings of shock and reaction. The loss of what was almost definitely an enormous poensie (60, 70 lbs?) still haunts me today. Writing this particular story has not been fun. I had made such a fundamental error in that battle that I deserved to cook for Tony for the rest of his life.

Some twenty years later my wife Judy, a talented portrait artist, asked me if I could pose with a look of anguish.

"A look of anguish? No problem dear. I have just the thing welded into my memory…"

We still have the portrait.

On the last morning of that trip, Tony had moved away from Table Rock to throw a spoon for kob or some shad for bait. It was still dark and after some time I made out Tony's voice shouting: GAFF…….GAFFFF……..*GAFFFFFFFFF!*

Left: *The author fishing Table Rock at Mbolompo, in an 'active' sea.*

I grabbed my gaff and sprinted towards where his headlamp was flashing wildly in my direction. When I arrived panting, I found him playing a good fish. He'd evidently been calling for some time as his voice was hoarse.

"Where've you been? I've been yelling and flashing for ages! Anyway, I can't risk bringing it in until it gets lighter."

So we waited some twenty odd minutes while the sun's first light glowing beyond the horizon gathered strength. One has to *work* for one's fish from the rocks...not like from a boat...!

All the while the fish stayed right on the surface, swinging from left to right, and keeping obligingly clear of the rocks. Finally Tony was able to guide his captive towards a suitable landing site. With the help of a wave the fish was lifted without difficulty into a good gaffing position in a relatively safe rock pool and I was able to do the honours. The catch was totally unexpected – a 25 lb barracuda (*Sphyraena japonica*), a delightfully unusual catch.

Right: *Tony's 25 lb 'cuda.*

On this, just my first trip, I had been well and truly initiated into the ups and downs, highs and lows, adrenalin pumping excitement and damned hard work of this utterly magnificent place. I would make quite a number of superb trips before sadly leaving it behind for Australian shores. If

I could have fitted it in with my luggage it would certainly have come with me!

During my first stay in Zululand I also had the opportunity to travel south and revisit another Transkei Wild Coast venue, an old family holiday haunt – Coffee Bay. This delightfully scenic part of the world boasted two hotels, one fancy and one 'family'. My absolute favourite was the family one, the Lagoon Hotel, owned and run by the wonderfully hospitable Ventriss family. The trip in question was the longest fishing holiday I have ever taken: four magical weeks. The Ventrisses were fishing-oriented and understood my solitary nocturnal habits well. They even made overnight sandwich packs for me, a great luxury for a bachelor.

Late one afternoon I set off to a very promising spot called Hlungwana, a small sugarloaf-like hill a few kilometres north of Coffee Bay. Unfortunately this enormously 'fishy' looking deep-water spot turned out to look better than it performed, at least as far as big fish were concerned. On this day I threw a spoon into the bay to the north of Hlungwana in the hope of …well… anything that was stupid enough to eat tin, and on that day an 11.5 lb skipjack (*Elops saurus*) obliged. These fellows were common enough, particularly when the water was very warm. However eleven point five pounders were not; they usually ran much smaller. All sizes were extremely likely to throw a lure – especially a heavy spoon – within seconds of taking it, almost inevitably ensured by repeated jumps and violent head shaking.

This fellow got unlucky, and despite an impressive display, ended up safely in the bag. I was very pleased. These fish are poor eating and better returned alive; however, provided they are used very fresh, their fillets are exceptionally good bait for kob. That was why I was pleased. If one wants to seriously target big kob with fillet, then good quality fresh bait of generous proportions, preferably still quivering and dripping blood, is essential. Shad is just as outstanding, also provided it is fresh. Unfortunately both species turn to mush very quickly after death. I was planning to chase kob that night and this was the very ticket. I had just one problem. The specimen was so big that it deserved a photograph for the record. I also needed it for bait. What to do?

Well, years of fishing had made me innovative if nothing else. I carefully filleted half of the fish cleanly from the backbone and left the other half intact for photographic purposes. As it turned out I needn't have bothered to fillet in the first place. Someone took a photograph that night before I went out. The fish in the photo is actually half a fish, held very carefully to hide the fact. (See below.) After the photographic session, I made my way to 'the Slide'.

Above: *The photogenic half of the*
11.5 lb skipjack used for bait.

The Slide: difficult to get to, bad to climb down and totally abominable to climb up, even without a fish. The path is called 'the Slide' because it is very steep, made of shale and the shale does just that – it slides, as do many people climbing up or down it. This was the spot at which fate, for some twisted reason, decided to deliver my biggest fish. I shouldn't really be surprised, should I?

The fishing spot itself can be seen in the photo below.

Previous page: *Showing the fishing area accessed via the Slide, on the far side of the chimney-like column of rocks just touching the water, located approximately on the horizontal centreline of the picture. The Slide itself is situated on this side of the light coloured triangle of rock with a dark shadow, jutting out in the bottom right hand corner of the photograph. Note the rough, slightly discoloured water – perfect for kob.*

Upon arrival in the dark at about 10.00 pm to catch the turn of the high tide, I rigged a heavy outfit – a Conolon rod modified to my personal taste and a Penn 49 'A' reel, with a slab of skipjack fillet on two 8/0 or 9/0 hooks. Kob have maws that would shock Jonah. For this reason, not only are big hooks not a problem, they are preferable, especially in a bait weighing over half a pound (226-plus grams to modernists). In my experience, kob are inclined to grab a very fresh fillet with far less hesitation than they will a live-bait. For this reason, and the fact that hooks very easily pull out of a kob's mouth during the fight, my preference is to use two hooks in a big bait. I was careful to make sure the points of the two hooks were well exposed – though not the hooks themselves.

Out went the bait with the usual big-bait heave. As can be seen from the photograph, the area is quite shallow. In even moderately rough weather, a strong sideways flow produced a noticeable pull on heavy line, but shale and small rocks on the bottom prevented the sinker from moving. I parked my bottom on the most comfortable outcrop of rock I could find and settled in for a long wait.

It was an unusually comfortable rocky parking place, for which reason I was quite pleased to sit and relax for a while after the walk, and for which reason it would also have to be that a fish bit almost immediately. Bit? More like inhaled the bait and swallowed. Hell, my backside had only just begun to take the shape of the rock I was perched on and I was on my feet again – in no uncertain terms. I wasn't even able to strike decently before it took off. It pulled like an express train, with such force that I was having a great deal of trouble maintaining my balance on the rock upon which I was standing. Fifty pound line was ripped from the spool as the fish took dangerous advantage of the sea's strong flow to the right. It was pitch dark and my vivid memory is of line disappearing into that darkness and the sense of a large fish rapidly increasing the distance between it and me. Very worrisome indeed.

To make things worse, I couldn't make my way along the rocks parallel with the movement of the fish – just too difficult in the dark. No choice but to put as much pressure on it as possible or run out of line. I did so, and kept up the pressure, arms already aching from using such a long heavy rod against such a weight. Eventually, against the unrelenting pull of my repeated attempts to turn it, the fish gave way, turned, and line recovery could commence. The fight continued for a long time. Every inch of regained line had to be won back against fish and current, with gains repeatedly being lost to the flick of a huge tail and another run in the opposite direction. My arms ached and shook with the relentless exertion.

The fish continued to use the currents to maximum advantage, but the runs eventually became shorter as time passed. My arms rejoiced at the declining fight but I still cursed the way the leverage of the very long rod worked against them. Long fights are fine on sandy beaches, but they are nerve-wracking off rocks and positively scary off rocks at night.

My nerves hovered constantly between severe apprehension and horror every time there was an untoward movement or other perceived threat to the connection between fish and me. Only *actual loss* feels worse. A *lot* worse. As always, the concern produced extreme concentration and caution. Every possible skill was applied: giving a little line when pushed, taking a little when possible, never forcing the issue, and constantly checking the drag to ensure a safe level of tension, loosening it slightly as the fish got closer. Landing big fish under these circumstances is demanding and hard work, but enormously rewarding when it works out.

The fish was approaching – time to look down the line with the headlamp and try to spot it. Frequent smallish swells were rolling in and crunching down fairly close to the rocky shore. The light beam lit up rows of sixty to ninety centimetre high broken waves against a near-black background (no moon), running in over, and petering out amongst, large smooth round boulders. Round and smooth that is, except for the areas of colonies of line-cutting barnacles and oysters which were poised in readiness to sabotage my efforts. These rocks lay ominously between the fish and me. Where to guide it in? This was where the rod's length would become advantageous. Casting, keeping the line clear of rocks, and guiding the fish, especially during these last stages, were the benefits of length.

I jumped precariously from rock to rock to best position myself to encourage the fish through the least threatening parts of that rocky gauntlet. I was now shaking more from excitement than fatigue, my eyes glued to where the nylon entered the water. My memory of the first sighting is still vivid – a great silver head with large pink eyes glowing in the light beam. That confirmed that it was a kob. That it was big was already obvious.

Unable to contain myself, and having no gaff, I made my way amongst the boulders into the water. I had to fight to maintain my balance, all the time keeping the line clear of cutting surfaces and taking any opportunity to use incoming waves to encourage the fish closer. At one stage I slipped, fell and vaguely felt barnacles against my shins. Ignoring this I got up again, regained tension on the line, and worked my way towards the fish which was now semi-stranded amongst the boulders.

After a total of about thirty minutes – though it felt more like forever – I was close enough to slide a hand hastily but *very* carefully under the base of a gill, and drag the fish to safety. The relief was intense. I couldn't believe its size. My previous record was broken, but I had no idea by how much. I was ecstatic, but also so exhausted I didn't even try another bait. I must have been nearly dead not to do that.

Instead I packed my gear and began the gruelling journey back to the top of the Slide. The fish was too big and awkward to carry over the rocks so I had to drag it. Upon arrival at the base of the Slide I found there was absolutely no way I could haul both my gear and the fish up it together. Not wishing to risk damage by feral dogs at the top, I left the fish at the bottom, and carried my gear up first, then climbed back down again. The fish came next and after inch-by-inching it up the Slide, all the time fighting against slipping back down, I was seriously stuffed by the time I got to the top, at around 1.00 am. I felt physically ill, and for the first time saw that the tops of my socks were absolutely soaked with blood. My shins had been quite badly ripped by barnacles when I fell – thank God they got me and not the line!

With considerable effort I lifted the fish into the back of the bakkie and drove down the hill, through the freshwater stream, and back to the hotel. The fish could spend the night in the vehicle – I didn't even have the energy to weigh it. I bandaged my shins (see photo) and hit the sack. Next morning the fish was hoisted up and tipped the hotel's scale at 66 lb – my biggest by far at the time, and an edible fish weight I have not managed to better to this day. I have from time to time wondered what the overnight drip-loss-factor from the fish might have been.

Above: *66 lb kob, Coffee Bay, 1977.*
Note bandaged shins.

I also had my second close encounter of the wrong kind with Mother Ocean at this same venue, again fishing alone. King Neptune sent a large wave as I was trying to free my trace from some mussels at the end of a short rocky promontory. It was night time, pitch dark and I was depending on my miner's headlamp to see my way around. All of a sudden, out of the black, an ominous rising shape loomed, barely visible. SHIT! It rose over the rock – and into me – before I could even turn, let alone retreat to safety. The water engulfed me and pushed me with such force that all grip was lost. As it fell back I went with it and felt the rock beneath me disappearing into seemingly bottomless sea with nothing to grab onto. In the black of night in a turbulent sea, this is a *very* uncomfortable sensation. With rod still tightly in my grip (a rod in the hand is better than nothing at all and I probably couldn't have let go if I'd tried), I trod water while I tried to get my bearings.

My headlamp had washed off my head but was safely attached to the rechargeable battery hanging on my belt. It was a miners' lamp, and the very heavy battery itself was trying - quite successfully - to pull me under. As the water receded from this higher than usual swell, I felt my feet touch terra oh-so-firma; very fortunately indeed this was not a particularly deep area. How good did *THAT* feel? 'KING good! I could just make out the rock from which I had been washed, very close by, and I struggled towards it, and then along next to it, still taking periodic dunkings from new swells, but only occasionally losing my footing very briefly. I clawed frantically at the water with my free arm until at last I reached shallower round boulders and was able to clamber out onto beautiful dry rock once again.

I was that spooked I reckon I was glowing white through my dripping clothes. Amazingly my lamp was still working – those miners' lamps were made for rougher treatment than that. I packed my gear and hauled myself out of there quick-smart. I knew that a mishap was always a possibility with my style of fishing and I knew I had had another close call. I felt rather like a half-drowned dog, and no doubt looked like one too. How to sneak back into the hotel unseen?

In September 1988 while still in Zululand, my family and I moved to live in the delightful seaside town of Mtunzini. From there I continued to visit Mbolompo (as described in the next chapter), but when I couldn't get there, Mtunzini stepped in and delivered some very pleasant fish. But before getting to them, it was in Mtunzini just a year or two before leaving for Australia, that I met a fellow by the name of Julian Pybus who fished competitively, in particular targeting large rays off the beach. What boggled my mind was his cast. He could throw a substantial fillet bait further than I had ever seen anyone throw anything before – further than I would have thought possible if I hadn't seen it with my own eyes. My own casting wasn't bad, but whenever I watched him perform, I felt like slinking off into the bushes somewhere and sulking with my tail between my legs. One day I put my pride in my pocket, walked over, introduced myself and asked him how the hell he did it. He pointed to his reel. Considering the bulk and weight of the baits he was throwing it looked relatively compact and light.

"Shimano SpeedMaster," he said, offering no more information, but with a knowing sort of a look.

He did sing its praises more comprehensively later, but by then he was preaching to the converted – I owned my own. It propelled me instantly into a new age of technology. It wasn't that my reels hadn't performed faithfully and well up until then; they had, it's just that by comparison they seemed to come out of the Stone Age. It has to be admitted, mind you, that as a married man I didn't upgrade my tackle *quite* as often as I had when a bachelor. At the time of writing, that first SpeedMaster that I bought is still going strong after some twenty years of service and has been passed on to my son. I currently own two more of them myself, with a fourth in the planning stage: "...Sweetheart, I really need another reel..."

Interestingly their very high gear ratio (6-1) makes them perfect for throwing a spoon, a great pleasure of mine.

Mtunzini's beautifully scenic estuary yielded some very nice kob of the 10 to 12 lb mark which could be quite plentiful at times, but I was far happier to discover an annual run of leervis (called garrick in Natal).

Left: *One of Mtunzini's beach leervis (garrick). These fish are reasonably similar to Australia's queenfish, but are heavier in the body.*

They prefer moderately clean water, something of a rarity in the sea in that area due to the regular flooding of rivers. This, along with the problem of strong side-wash on all but the very calmest days, meant that opportunities to target them were anything but plentiful. Nevertheless perseverance prevailed, and using live mullet caught in the estuary, I landed some good-sized fish from the beach.

On one early morning excursion I had two lines out. (I had a habit of asking for trouble.) The rods were perched in rod holders stuck into the sand, ratchets on and drags set only just tight enough to stop the side-wash from taking line. Each was baited with a live mullet. Before too long, one mullet was picked up in a run that suggested the eater was desperately hungry and that there was some competition for food out there. It tore off up the beach. As luck would have it, it collected the second line in the process, leaving me wondering how on earth I could separate the two. It has always been a mystery to me how something apparently so uncomplicated can end up in such an almighty tangle of line.

I played the fish for quite some time. Playing big fish from a beach is an absolute breeze compared with the rocks, as there are usually no hazards. This means that light line can be used, and fish allowed to run without any critical need to hold them hard. Leervis are in any case absolute gentlemen, usually fighting totally cleanly and on the surface. When I landed the fish I discovered an unpleasant mess of nylon from the second rod, around the fish. It must have been quite dizzy judging by the number of circles which would have been needed to create such a disaster.

What was more intriguing is that there was obviously more than a live mullet at the end of this second line. A lot more! I have no idea when the second mullet was picked up by a fish, but it certainly had been. And whatever had picked it up was hooked and protesting strongly against the inconvenience. There was no way I could reel it in, so it had to be pulled in by hand. This took considerable time and effort, including avoiding getting caught up in or tripping over the tangled mess of line, and being forced periodically to relinquish line every time the fish took the upper hand. The process was made even more complex by the obvious necessity to disguise my ridiculous predicament from fellow anglers passing by in their vehicles. It is not easy to fight a twenty pound fish on a hand-line in such a way as to suggest nothing strange or suspicious is happening, though picking one's nose with a free finger helps to divert attention and send would-be observers on their way.

After a considerably longer battle than the first, the second fish was eventually landed. They were both beauties in the early and mid twenty pounds. Fortunately not all of my catches involved such complications, but Mbolompo, rugged rock formations and night fishing, wasn't always simple either…

Right: *The two leervis, with a small kob from the night before.*

Chapter 7

Mbolompo: Fisherman's Paradise! More Big Fish, Another Hook in the Hand, Doggy Misdemeanors, Bribery, and Stories of Some Fishy Characters

Having taken the liberty of referring to the place as paradise, let me open the chapter with a story to demonstrate why I did so. The year was 1981, it was my second or third trip to Mbolompo, and the day was magnificent – not only because it was windless, warm blue

Above: *Mbolompo point in the distance, (the last narrow point of land on the extreme left) with Lubanzi beach and our tents and vehicles at lower right next to the sandy river mouth – a considerable distance to carry big fish.*

sky'd and calm sea'd, but because I had just been fortunate enough to land a big fish, hence successfully completing the angler's infamous 'Great Chain of Events'. (Infamous because there is so often a link missing, causing a fish to be lost, or not connected with in the first place.) The Great Chain in this case entailed being in the right place at the right time; having the desired bait – on this occasion a live shad (tailor); casting its 1 lb vigorously flapping body to the desired spot; having it stay in place *and* alive (not drifting or swimming into the rocks) until the right predator came along and consumed it; timing the strike; setting the hooks; keeping the fish away from any rocky escape routes, and finally after a gargantuan battle successfully extracting it from the depths.

It was a lucky day. As every fisherman knows, each link in rock-fishing's Great Chain of Events is fragile. King Neptune works frantically and unerringly on behalf of the fish, endeavouring to free it by means of big waves, sharp rocks, broken knots etc, lending bitter truth to the angler's idioms 'many a slip twixt hook and fish's lip', and 'a fish in the bag is worth thousands in the sea'.

To add to my ego-satisfaction, on this particular day there happened to be several spectators – a relatively rare event in those days, as the location was one of the Transkei's more isolated spots. I deposited my 40 lb 'poensie' (black steenbras) in a suitably large rock pool for its safe keeping, well back from Neptune's thieving waves. As the catch was carefully deposited in its pool, one of the spectators – a large and imposing figure – made his way towards me. Despite having the appearance of one not easily impressed, he was obviously unable to control his bulging eyeballs. He stared, silent but definitely moved. Eventually he looked at me almost expressionlessly (except for the eyes) and said,

"JISLAAAIK, maar dis nou 'n *man* se vis, daai!" ("CRIKEY, but that's now a *man's* fish, that one!")

Well, I can tell you I felt pretty darn good in that moment – worth all the blood, sweat and tears of other fish*less* fishing efforts. The fish was damned good eating too, even if a spade was needed to remove its armour-like scales.

Above: *"That's a MAN'S fish, that!"* *A 40 lb
poensie (black steenbras,* Cymatoceps nasutus*)
caught using live shad (tailor) for bait,
Mbolompo, July 1981.*

Having once tasted Mbolompo, I made every effort to
visit as regularly and often as possible, which meant if I
were lucky, a seven to ten day trip once a year for most
years. There were so many wonderful and colourful events
experienced at Mbolompo, it is difficult to choose which to
recount. The first which comes to mind is not even fishy. It
is about the washing facility. For people that is, not the
dishes. Who would bother to wash dishes on a fishing trip?

The most convenient option for washing when we camped at Lubanzi was a shallow, blind, and usually slightly brackish stream close to the camp, visible just below and to the right of the tents in the photograph. Convenient does not mean comfortable. We often visited Mbolompo in July – midwinter – when the air temperature could be close to frosty. On those occasions the 'bath water' would be cold enough to freeze the monkeys off a brass ball. (Yeah, yeah I know, but it was colder than that!) A fresh breeze off the hills did nothing to help, and drying oneself in the wind was a numbing experience which was carried out, like the washing, with blinding speed and only moderate success. A further irritation was the outright refusal of the soap to lather in the water which was either too hard, too salty, or both. Never mind, that was a good excuse not to use soap.

Actually, all things considered (except for one's fishing mates, that is), it was better not to wash at all. And even considering one's fishing mates, if everyone stuck to the practice there should be no problem, or at least the problem would be equally shared. My best achievement in this regard was seven straight days without washing. I always tell the story with pride. I have told it to many, and invariably the listener's look is one of being considerably impressed, perhaps even a touch jealous. You know – that upturned face, pinched eyes, tight mouth and wrinkled nose – an unmistakable look of envy.

It was not only washing in the cold that presented a problem. It could be so chilly in the wee-wee hours of the morning that the old urinary private part would withdraw in horror when exposed to it. On a bad night it would do this to the extent that shaking off the last drop of amber liquid (no, not beer, though sometimes probably quite close to it) would be impossible, and the return trip to the tent would have the added delight of a cold wetness on the inside of one tracksuit leg.

Right: *The Lubanzi 'bath tub'.*

Mbolompo does not hold happy memories for everyone in my family. I took my (very new) wife there to introduce her to the *real* benefits of married life. It took some considerable effort to persuade her that camping was one such benefit. Actually I didn't really manage to persuade her about the delights of camping before embarking on the first trip, but she agreed to at least try it.

To make things easier, we went with the largest group of people I have ever been there with, including her sister's family and several friends. The weather was foul. It blew and rained, and rained and blew. She was not amused. Fish for the pot were scarce, and opportunities for walks on the beach and suchlike even more scarce. We lived in the back of my bakkie (ute) under its canopy, which after allocating a little space for food and clothing etc and a great deal for fishing tackle, didn't leave much room for comfort.

When weather permitted I tried to appease her by introducing her to the cultural interests of the area. For example, I showed her a group of Xhosa women (the local tribe) who came down to the sea to give each other enemas. The process was conducted by getting the subject (victim?) to kneel, and covering her with a blanket. This special blanket was equipped with a hole which was then appropriately positioned so as to provide orificial access. A cow's horn was modified for the purpose by cutting off the tip to give a hole at each end, one large and one small. The narrow end was inserted into the orifice in question. Sea water from a suitable receptacle was then decanted into the bowel via the horn. The reverse cycle, then including solids, presumably followed shortly after.

The process was repeated until all six or seven women had been purged in this way. Whatever became of the 'purge poop' I am not certain, as I didn't look very hard to find out. I expect the Transkei's roaming 'night-cart-brigade' in the form of plump little black pigs, dealt with it. They took their duties very seriously and could often be seen trotting around snouting away, looking for the daily doings of any donors.

A few days after this cultural highlight had been watched from a distance comfortable to both parties, our seven year old nephew came bouncing into camp one morning, blowing away enthusiastically on a cow's horn he'd picked up in the grass, proudly producing sounds very reminiscent of a series of vibrant, voluminous farts.

A few quick words in his ear and my last recollections of the incident were of the nephew in question running screaming down the hill towards the stream to wash his mouth out.

We made just one more attempt at a family visit to the Wild Coast some years later, to M'Kambati, this time with two young sons, one in nappies, one just out. It blew and rained, and rained and blew, and we went home early…

Before returning to fishing, and before you pack your bags to visit the area, here's a final story depicting the flavour of the place. This story revolves around the famous 'Transkei Trots'. Oh no, it's not about tribal tradition or indigenous dancing. It's not even about horses. In fact it has to do with bowel movement rather than leg movement, though the legs do admittedly play an important part in getting to a suitable venue. To get the bowel moving in the way that the story describes, one needs to make a fundamental error. I made two in this instance; the first an old familiar one, which led to number two – literally and figuratively…

The first mistake I made on this occasion was to neglect to take clean drinking water with me on a fishing outing. Just for a change… The second mistake was to stick my face into a small pool in a local stream (creek) of seemingly innocent and delectably cool water. 'Seemingly' innocent, because I didn't allow my thoughts to go to the additives which were almost guaranteed to have found their way into the water. Think cow poo, goat poo, pig poo, and of course enema poo. *No way* did I let my thoughts go there – hell, if I had, I wouldn't have been able to *touch* it, and I was damned thirsty. So I sucked with oblivious thirst-quenching pleasure and a day or so later the belly rumbling, body-contorting cramps and supersonic squirts began.

Exactly which anti-social micro-organisms are responsible I wouldn't have a clue. I am more experienced in the symptoms, which are violent and unrelenting. For reasons unknown to me, this common and well-known ailment most often struck me on the road trip home, where its magnitude – as measured by urgency, frequency, pressure and volume – was most easily expressed in terms of toilet-rolls-per-ten-kilometres of travel. Many a small shrub got well fertilized; bigger shrubs could not always be found in time.

On this occasion however, as luck would have it, the first explosion occurred just before I left for a late afternoon/night fishing shift. As a result, while Tony Simpson pressed on to Mbolompo point itself, probably chuckling away to himself that there was an excellent chance that I would end up doing the cooking next day, the best I could do was to hobble, body bent and buttocks clenched as far as Black Rock.

Well, I needn't have worried. My belief that life is inherently balanced was vindicated that night, though admittedly with some difficulty. Black Rock delivered a 47 lb kob. Of course carrying it back wasn't much fun, but life's balance understandably consists of ups and downs. I suspect the actual overall balance only becomes evident – if we are very lucky – on the day we kark it. Right then I was quite happy with life's balance in the moment. Fish rule!

Above: *The 47 lb kob, caught 'under pressure'. The two smaller kob were caught the following morning on spoon. By that time, after considerable involuntary action on my part, my bowel had jet-propelled itself back to pristine cleanliness, and normality reigned once more.*

Back to purely fishing matters, sharks were an occasional feature at Mbolompo, sometimes invited, sometimes not. Cold water tended to bring about their uninvited arrival in large numbers. Tony and I were fishing there one morning in a cold grey sea. The sea was thick with 'raggies' (ragged tooth sharks, *Carcharius taurus*) averaging, when judged by our fishing efforts, between 100 and 200 lb in weight. I landed one which we estimated at about 175 lb. This was lifted onto Table Rock, photographed showing its toothy grin, (see below) and returned alive. They are not particularly vigorous fighters, and this specimen was easily handled out of water, apart from its weight, that is.

Above: *Ragged tooth shark estimated at 175 lb – returned alive after photographing.*

At one stage Tony released a specimen of perhaps 125 lb, which swam off close to the surface. Suddenly a piccanin (young Xhosa boy), sitting on the high rock just behind Table Rock, let out a yell. We nearly fell off the rock in surprise – what could he be on about? Unfortunately neither of us spoke more than a few words of Xhosa, but eventually we were able to extract from him the fact that he had seen a monster shark rise up and attack the released shark from underneath. Judging by his scream and subsequent rapid babble, and the size of the released shark, it must have been a monster.

The *invited* sharks, on the other hand, were intentionally sought using a specially designed kite rig which was used to carry a large bait several hundred metres out, where it was supported near to the surface by a plastic bottle half filled with water. The water in the bottle stopped the kite from lifting the bait out of the water while the air in the empty half stopped the bait from sinking. Some enthusiasts attempt to set the weight of water such that the bait lifts and falls back periodically, its splash providing a strong attraction to predators.

I would settle for a bait fish of at least two pounds, but the more serious shark fishermen preferred far bigger baits. I used a Penn Senator 14/0 holding about 1000 metres of 80 lb nylon. A bait line was attached to the main line, some distance away from the kite. This dropped vertically into the sea. A black marker was fastened about centrally on the bait line. This would plunge towards the sea when the bait was taken – very exciting. Basically, the shark swimming against the pull of the kite seemed to set the hooks, and the kite then provided a useful amount of shark-fighting energy. When the wind was favourable I would fish with a kite during the day when fishing for edibles was at its poorest. Though no giants presented themselves, it was an interesting exercise, and some reasonable specimens were landed. They were always returned alive after a photographic session and appeared totally unaffected, judging by their vigorous swim for freedom when released.

Right: *Playing a shark on a kite rig, including a harness.*

Left: *the shark*

My preference though, was always for edibles, and on one Mbolompo trip I experienced a 48 hour fishing period that one normally only dreams of. The first fish attacked a tin spoon well after sundown on the first day, in what we called Tegwan Bay; 'tegwan' being the Xhosa name for the well known and easily recognisable 'hammerkop' bird. Tegwan Bay is superbly fishable in a strong south westerly blow as this roughens up the sea very suitably for kob on spoon and one is throwing approximately with the wind.

Interestingly it took some time for this fish to wake up and start to fight with the weight and power it had at its disposal. For a fair while it felt like an average fish, maybe fifteen or twenty pounds, but eventually it woke up and I wised up. When I realized its considerable size I decided to make my way over the rocks by torchlight to the sandy beach and land it there rather than on the rocks where it had been hooked. Kob are heavy and strong but not wildly active fighters, which made this fairly precarious journey possible in the dark. Fortunately I had put on my miner's head lamp earlier as soon as the light faded, and didn't have to wrestle to get this on while playing the fish.

The fish probably took at least forty minutes of very careful fighting on spinning tackle before it could be beached, which finale, though the rocky walk to the beach in the dark was tricky, was far more easily conducted than a rocky landing. The fish was a kob weighing 58 lb.

Above: *58 lb kob, caught on a tin spoon in the dark at Tegwan Bay.*

I had to carry it to the top of the hill overlooking Mbolompo, and not via the usual 'easier' though longer beach route to Lubanzi camp. Man, what a haul in the dark! To say that I was knackered by the time I reached the top would be a lie. I was severely fornicated. I lay on my back for some time to stop my heart from attacking me. At the time, I figured both the fish and I deserved to be immortalised in wax at Madame Tussaud's.

That didn't happen. Instead we smoked the fish to preserve it, but unfortunately the maggots decided they also liked smoked fish, and much had to be discarded later. The local piccanins – young Xhosa boys of seven or eight years of age – observing the goings-on at the time, fared better. After pieces suitable for smoking had been removed, they were given the head (a delicacy) and other unused parts to eat. Interestingly, as they cooked their pieces of fish on a fire, they repeatedly dipped these in the fish's raw visceral fluids as they cooked them. For them this 'sauce' seemed to be king's fare. Not for me thanks!

Very early the next morning, in the dark, Tony and I headed back to Tegwan for a quick spoon-throwing session to test the waters before heading off to the point to look for poensies (black streenbras). A few throws later I hooked, subdued and landed a 30 pound kob, which I placed alive in a large rock pool. Tony caught a shad (tailor) or two which he kept for bait. Ten or so throws later I was into a fish again. The sun had either just risen or was about to. I could make the fish out fighting lazily near the surface – not that it wasn't pulling hard; it was, but it wasn't thrashing about. After a hard but clean fight of perhaps ten or fifteen minutes, a 25 lb leervis was subdued, landed and placed in the pool with the kob.

Tony caught another shad or two, muttering something about their nuisance value when bigger fish were around. Incredibly, while he caught more shad I caught another two leervis of 24 and 38 lb each. I even cut off the actual spoon I was using and gave it to him, but it was one of those inexplicable occasions where one person catches and another doesn't.

Above: *Two home-made tin 'spoons' of the design used for catching the fish in this story – and many others – showing the flat side with a 'suicide' hook (top spoon) and convex section (bottom spoon). Metal length: 100 mm; weight: 80 grams. As can be seen from the photograph, the soft metal gets dented easily when retrieved over rocks.*

Left: *38, 24 and 25 lb leervis.*

Right: *30 lb kob, with the 38 lb dead leervis against the rock.*

At this stage Tony said he was going to the point and started to pack. I said I would have a few more throws at Tegwan and suggested that considering the circumstances, he should actually be going back to camp to cook my breakfast. While Tony was muttering something uncomplimentary, I sent my spoon on another piscatorial assignment.

Third or fourth throw and 'whack', I was into yet another fish. Tony was still watching, but unfortunately I was concentrating on not being pulled into the sea. I would have loved to have seen his face – I reckon both his face and his mutterings would have been pretty interesting at this latest unfolding.

This fish was clearly not a leervis, though just what it was I couldn't guess. It tore off towards the opposite side of the bay at breakneck (and line!) speed, leaving me trying every trick in the book to quieten it down. Only the opposite side of the bay seemed to stop it. Fortunately, for some unknown reason it didn't head out to sea or it would certainly have stripped the Penn 49 (narrow version of the 49 'A') of its less than 200 metres of 40 lb line.

From this position it fought a sustained, extremely strong and active fight, showing no signs of weakening for a considerable time. Its power to streak off at leisure made my spinning outfit feel horribly underpowered, but most fortunately at no time did it seem inclined to head out to the open sea and freedom. When it was eventually time to consider landing it, as with the big kob of the night before, I decided to try to reach the beach for an easier landing. This was considerably simpler in the daylight, even with a far more powerful fight on my hands. By the time I reached the beach, the fish was probably still 40 to 50 metres away, but I was progressively gaining ground. It swam from side to side, very effectively using the length of its body, side on, to slow its retrieval. I got glimpses of it but could still not identify it.

Finally the fish lifted in a peaking swell and I got my first view of its cigar shaped body gliding along sideways in front of me. A YELLOWTAIL! (Kingfish to Aussies.) *SHOOT!* What a dream fish. I couldn't believe it. The beauty of this magnificent specimen cruising along the tops of clear turquoise swells over a sandy bottom in the early morning sunlight was beyond words. I soaked it in, enraptured.

Cautiously I reduced pressure, loosening the drag slightly, and prepared for the final stages. Provided there was no last minute mishap, there was no reason to expect trouble. Or so I thought. As the fish drew closer into shallower water, there was a splashing behind me and a piccanin who had brought my gaff along rushed past me, slashing wildly at the fish with the gaff in an attempt to hook it. Once again my heart threatened to attack me, and being insufficiently acquainted with the native tongue, I made loud noises of a universally understood kind. They were quickly understood, the gaff was withdrawn, and my nerves settled down marginally.

That incredible fish simply refused to give up. Every inch of ground gained in the slowly reducing arcs in front of me was hard won. Still powerful dashes for freedom continued to the end, until I was finally able to carefully lift the huge body and carry it to the rock pool housing the other four fish. It tipped the scale at 50 lb. Unfortunately the 38 lb leervis had died. We photographed the other four fish alive and returned them successfully to the sea.

The leervis was smoked a lot more satisfactorily than the big kob, its oily fillets turning out to be quite delicious when smoked using the dried leaves of a local shrub. We salted them more heavily and the creepy crawlies were kept at bay, hopefully to their great annoyance – pestiferous little varmints!

Above: *50 lb yellowtail (*Seriola lalandi – *kingfish in Australia) with the 38 lb leervis which died, in the background. The yellowtail was returned alive after photographing.*

Left: *The 26 lb kob of the third morning. Note the narrow Penn 49 reel, with which all seven fish were landed.*

Above: *Tegwan Bay. The fish described above were all caught from the rocky point on the far side of the bay, situated 'under' the tip of the fishing rod held by the young Xhosa boy. Table Rock is amongst the rocky outcrop, visible a little further round, to the right. (Photo courtesy of Mike Thom.)*

The fun wasn't over yet: the following morning another kob of 26 lb was added to the collection. In all, I had caught seven fish weighing a total of 251 lb and having an average individual weight of nearly 36 lb each. I sincerely doubt my chances of beating that catch off the rocks in this lifetime, though it could have happened while catching giant trevally off a beach in Queensland Australia some years later, when the decision was made to stop because enough had been caught.

A most remarkable aspect of that Wild Coast fishing session was how Tony's catches, even using the actual spoon that I had been using, were limited to shad only, while I didn't catch one shad. How are such things explained? I certainly don't know.

A few days later Tony and I were spinning from the same spot, standing right next to each other. All of a sudden: 'SMACK!' Something travelling at high speed hit me plumb in the centre of my shoulders and bounced off, only to flop back and dangle from my clothing, attached by its treble hooks. "WHAT THE FFUUU...?"

Tony's tin spoon had caught me with a hard, though fortunately only glancing, blow on the back. Maybe it was punishment because my catches had seen him doing the cooking for the past few days and he was trying to upset my appetite and fishing ability.

Above: *The spoon-in-the-back episode.*

It is now time to introduce another Mbolompo personality, Mike Thom: co-angler, co-camper, chief photographer and occasional shit-stirrer. This book, and indeed my fishing trips to the Transkei would have been vastly less colourful, interesting and fun without him.

When I first met Mike in Eshowe, KwaZulu-Natal, he was busy working on something for which he needed figures from the periodic table. I think that's what it's called! Anyway, it's the list of all of the elements and their atomic weights, not a fold-up camping utensil. In seconds I realized he knew the thing off by heart – elements, atomic numbers, weights and whatever else it contains. Sheeesh, and I occasionally boast my chemical prowess with puffed up chest by referring to water as H O 2, or whatever it is.

Above: *Mike Thom taking a serious photograph of some crayfish in a group under a tree.*

175

Mike's incredible knowledge extended far and wide: metallurgy, chemistry, bee keeping, snakes, mechanics, electronics, photography etc. I was never concerned when travelling with him in his ageing Land Rover – it might be slow, but you knew you would get to and back from your destination, even if it meant stripping the Landy to its last bolt on the side of the road and putting it back together again. I myself never contributed much during these mechanical interludes though I did occasionally try:

"What's this, Mike?" I would ask helpfully.

"It's a valve cap off somebody else's tube. Please press the brake *very* gently three times so I can get the air bubbles out of the brake fluid. Gently, GENTLY! Whoa! STOP! **STOP!** Too late. Ah well. I'll just have to begin again. Don't you have some fishing tackle that needs cleaning?"

A capitalized and italicised word was almost as strong as language got for Mike, so when it was bolded as well, I knew I was really in the dwang – severely reprimanded. Nothing for it but to slink off and throw stones at a nearby fence-post until he was finished. (My fishing tackle was cleaner than his jolly Landrover; worked better too – well, most of the time.)

But by far the most important thing about Mike was that he loved the outdoors, adventure and fishing. And of all his activities, his practices when engaged in fishing, were most unorthodox – even more unorthodox than the time when he was explaining how a snake would not bite a stationary object. He kept his left hand still while pulling a night-adder backwards away from it with his right hand. Quite understandably, the snake had no idea that it was itself and not Mike's left hand that was moving, and bit him. Not deadly, but very unpleasant – his arm swelled grotesquely and I'm sure that particular demonstration was never repeated.

Nor was Mike, by a very considerable margin, your standard stereotypical fisherman. However, I very soon learned not to make fun of his unusual fishing strategies.

"Mike, take a tip from an old man of the sea, you'll get bugger-all on that scrap of crayfish – the fish'll see the hook from a mile off. You need to cover it. And the hook's too small for the job as well, by the way. Anyway, it's 9.00 am and too late for action, lets go and have breakfast... "WHAT! I don't *believe* it! Hang on, hang on! I'll get the gaff..."

This is not a fictitious tale. The fish, a 20 lb kob, was successfully landed on the 'too small' hook, having eaten the miserable scrap of bait far later in the morning than it should have done. Of course it didn't know all these things, and went about its business regardless. I learned very quickly to expect not only the unlikely but the downright near impossible when fishing with Mike.

Some of Mike's other catches included a 20 lb poensie caught at night from a magnificent fishing spot called Black Rock, and a beautiful yellowtail of around 25 lb, also caught at night, from Table Rock at the point. Interestingly, the yellowtail was caught thanks to a totally serendipitous event. We had been given six precious pilchards by a (rare) departing fisherman. They were precious because our own supply had run out and being many miles on atrocious roads from the nearest supply, we weren't going to be getting any more in the near future.

We decided to keep them for use at night rather than waste them in the daytime. As it got dark we climbed onto Table Rock and prepared to launch them into a warm, fairly calm sea. I don't recall for sure who cast first, but knowing Mike's time-consuming, scientifically oriented preparatory habits, it was probably me. Within seconds of my first bait hitting the bottom it was grabbed without ceremony and the game was on. I had no idea what it could be but it was strong and lively, without showing any inclination to move to either side or go for the rocks. It fought hard and deep, but cleanly, and was brought to the gaff in the gully to the left of Table Rock without great difficulty. It was a yellowtail of 20-plus pounds.

This woke Mike up, and scientific preparation was immediately expedited, though not totally abandoned, of course. Within seconds of his bait hitting the bottom, he too was into a good fish, also a yellowtail, which he landed. I landed one more, we missed three more strikes, and that was the end of our pillies. Thereafter it was as though the sea was devoid of fish. Fresh shad fillets and live pinkies, which was all we had apart from our pillies, were totally ignored. This was not the only time such fastidiousness was observed. On occasion only live karanteen would be taken. Any other live-bait would be totally ignored, while a karanteen (*Sarpa salpa*) would be grabbed within seconds –

very frustrating when karanteen were scarce, which they so often were.

I have watched game fish (pelagics) circle less favoured live-baits such as black-tail (*Diplodus sargus*) suspended from a float, as though debating whether to take them. Very frustrating and adrenalin producing. Live shad and karanteen when available were very rarely refused, and certainly topped my list of live-bait preferences. Mullet would doubtless be taken just as enthusiastically, but were not available at the point.

Above: *Mike's 'night-time' yellowtail.*
Note the reel – he would definitely feel
at home in Australia.

Mike's scientific inclinations well and truly extended to his fishing. Amongst other things, I recall his involvement in the design of a gadget that worked by employing highly compressed air to blast one's bait over the horizon. There was heated discussion as to whether it should be called a 'sinker sender' or 'bait bazooka'. One of its remaining shortcomings when I last heard about it was that the bait was always completely annihilated in the process. Yep, not hard to see how that could be a problem!

I also recall many a frustrating occasion when I would yell, "Mike the fish are here, get a line in, man! They'll be gone soon!"

And the reply would come back, "I'm just testing these knots. It's amazing; I'm losing 20% of the line strength with one knot and nearly 40% with the other. I just want to retest and make sure. I used your fishing scale but the spring's a bit rusty – looks as though it's been filed at some time. I'll use mine, just need to oil it a bit. I'm going to test these swivels too – made in China ..."

What could you do? It didn't matter anyway; the fish were kind to Mike and exempted him from Neptune's normal rules which make sure we lose more than we catch – the same rules as were applied to me with full force and grim determination.

While Mike's fishing activities could on occasion be viewed as being assisted by a mystifying degree of luck, his talents in more land-based matters were beyond dispute. For example, his ability to negotiate us out of a very tight spot when we had forgotten (or not bothered) to acquire camping permits for the area, was frequently in demand. This could be tricky. Increasingly over the years, the power vested in the local Xhosa indunas (headmen) for ensuring that anglers had the correct permits for the area had become recognised for its trading value. And the indunas could be very stubborn, refusing to give ground if not satisfied with the way negotiations were going.

Mike, having had long exposure to such matters, knew what was needed and always ensured that we were well equipped to bargain. This meant a good supply of 'firewater'. While the actual brand of firewater was not of great consequence, its alcoholic strength most definitely was.

Generally, a few days after our arrival, the induna would be noticed some way off approaching on horseback, recognisable by a small entourage of piccanins who had doubtless made him aware of our presence. The bargaining-bottle would be dug out of hiding or unlocked from a vehicle and readied – not visible, but easily accessible. A very large baked enamel mug and a smaller drinking vessel would also be made available, plus a second smaller one if I were to join in.

As he approached, the induna would be greeted with a wave from me. I avoided using the few Xhosa words I did know for fear of inadvertently insulting him. Mike, more daringly, would offer a verbal greeting. The induna would nod gravely.

Above: *Let the bargaining begin! The 'upper' camp site, with Mbolompo Point in the distance. The Induna is dressed in hat and coat, ready for business. Note the fish smoker – the drum with a hessian sack draped over it.*

Big things were at stake here. We would be asked for our permit. If we had a valid one, a relatively small amount of negotiating would be sufficient – just a few mouthfuls to secure a good starting position for any future negotiations when we might *not* have the required paperwork.

The bottle would be brought out, appropriate amounts poured, and we would park ourselves on the ground. The negotiating fluid would be examined visually by the induna, swirled, given a judgemental sniff, then with a nod it would be slurped progressively from the large mug. Much sound would be generated with surprisingly little liquid being taken up with each suck. Periodic nods and gestures of approval would be offered – a good sign.

Even minor negotiations could take ages. Regardless of the initial volume, when finally emptied the mug would be held out in an unmistakable gesture for more – a universally understood piece of sign language. Sometimes we would oblige, sometimes not. Preferably we would not, for any remaining firewater could always be used by Mike and me to negotiate between ourselves at some later date.

More serious negotiations, like those dealing with an absence of the required paperwork, took longer, and Mike might invite the induna into the tent. Apart from a broad-grinned greeting and possibly a handshake, I would keep out of these affairs which were clearly too delicate for my cumbersome ways. There would be mutters from inside the tent and occasionally the induna's raised voice would issue forth. Mike's voice would never rise. As time passed the slurps would get longer, noisier and more frequent and the induna's voice would lower. Things would be nearing an amicable conclusion.

Eventually the two would emerge, both a little shaky. These negotiations needed to be fair and well balanced – totally unachievable without adequate alcoholic facilitation on both sides. Farewells would be conducted, and the induna would jump onto his horse, usually still with a serious expression, and ride away over the hills. If negotiations had been particularly tough, the induna would stagger out, attempt a few times to mount his horse, and failing this, would allow the trusty steed to lead him slowly and unsteadily home.

Occasionally we were able to secure a more long term status of acceptability by photographing the induna and presenting him with his own picture on a subsequent trip. This was indeed a powerful bargaining tool, though never to be used without a good dose of firewater as well, of course.

We never had a negative outcome. We always made sure there was sufficient firewater and film to reach agreement.

Occasionally, Mike would bring his magnificent German shepherd dog 'Pesi' (meaning 'lion' in the Sotho language) on our trips. Pesi would usually be tied to a tent pole while we were out fishing, and theft of food and fishing tackle would drop to an incredible zero. One day when Pesi had joined us on an actual fishing outing, we heard him barking excitedly in the distance. Mike leapt to his feet and tore off in the direction of the barking, while I took up the rear. As we approached the spot in the northern corner of a small bay bordered by Black Rock, the unmistakable bleating of a goat in distress became audible in between Pesi's barks. Mike's pace increased twofold. He knew what Pesi could do to a goat, and he knew the likely consequence – one almighty lot of negotiating of the most awkward kind.

Fortunately the goat was safe, albeit not happy. I have always thought goats to be perhaps slightly more blessed in the department of savvy than the rest of the domesticated four legged family – certainly more so than the bovine branch. This one had, quite correctly I'm sure, figured that drowning would be a pleasanter death by far than one delivered by Pesi's teeth. Accordingly, on the basis of this doubtless lightning-fast decision, it had launched itself off the rocks into a none too peaceful looking sea.

Immediately upon arriving on the scene and realizing what had happened, Mike ripped off his shoes and shirt and did likewise. He headed in the goat's direction, its salvation obviously uppermost in his mind. As I watched the animal's response to its would-be rescuer, my high estimates of goat savvy faded within seconds. It seemed to do everything possible to hinder Mike's efforts. (Mind you, they say humans do much the same when drowning.) Maybe it thought Mike was Pesi!

Fortunately Mike's mind must have kept repeating to him, "CONSEQUENCES, CONSEQUENCES,

CONSEQUENCES..." for he somehow overcame the thrashing hooves and flailing horns to drag the protesting creature shorewards.

Finally, both looking equally bedraggled, they reached the edge and could be helped out. Pesi was told to 'stay' and the goat took off as though 'stay' meant 'kill'. I shudder to think how many bottles of firewater or other barter items it may have taken to make that little problem go away if the goat hadn't been rescued.

Pesi wasn't only interested in goats. He was a full blooded male and there were plenty of dogs in the area, and hence one can reasonably assume, bitches too. Despite being a most handsome example of German Shepherdness, and the local dogs mere runts by comparison, I believe that like most dogs Pesi was also a gentleman and totally 'un-

class-conscious' when it came to matters of *amour*. He would simply not have had it in him to reject a bitch on account of low calibre.

Thoughts must constantly have crossed his mind while we were out fishing, but Pesi was an exceptionally well behaved and obedient dog and I was only once aware of any such amorous excursion. This was unmistakably evidenced one morning upon our return from fishing, by a missing tent pole and collapsed tent. There could be no other explanation for the use of such force. The wind was off the hills, and quite understandably, pheromonal invitations wafting into camp on the breeze must have proved too much for him.

Pesi went missing for a day and caused great concern in camp, but always with our underlying hope that it had been worth his trouble. If he was successful, and it was pretty likely he would have been, it would have been most interesting to witness the owner's response to the size of the resultant pups – he probably still has a look of utter disbelief on his face.

Mike tended to carry a set of tools with him even when he was fishing, and one morning this proved very fortunate for me. I was doing the early morning shift in East Wind Bay, and had landed a small kob of about 4 lb on a tin spoon. This spoon was equipped with a 'suicide' hook: a large single hook fastened to the top end of it, with the usual treble hook at the bottom. After lifting the flapping kob onto the rocks I made the incredibly dumb mistake of grabbing the spoon to pick it up with. It gave one vigorous flap and hey presto – we shared a common bond! The single hook had plunged its way deep into my hand. With considerable difficulty, not to mention great gobs of 'ouch factor', I managed to get the fish off the spoon. At least then I was only decorated with a large piece of 'jewellery' and wouldn't look quite so ridiculous – at least I hoped not.

I waited for the others to arrive; they were generally not so keen on the *very* early morning shift starting in the dark. Mike appeared on the path grinning broadly, in all likelihood anticipating the trial of some new piece of fishing gadgetry he had invented.

"Mike, I've got a bloody great hook in my hand," I advised him. He strolled over and put his gear down.

"Letsava look…YOHHHH! You're not kidding!" That was a strong reaction from Mike. For some reason he never swore. Never tried it I suppose, and never discovered what he was missing. It didn't matter – I always filled in for him.

"Don't worry, I'm sure I've got some wire cutters here," he said reassuringly as though this was to be expected. "Yep, here we are, hold out your hand."

The area close to the hook had hardened and gone white, and my hand in general had swollen and ached like hell. I wasn't looking forward to the exercise but I knew it had to be done. After all, I couldn't continue fishing with a spoon hanging from my hand, and this was the second part of the early shift – prime fishing time. Mike opened his cutters and positioned their jaws around the hook's shaft. The strain on his face told how tough the steel was, as did the expression on my own, I'm sure. I don't recall how the actual cutting felt, but it was a relief after the 'knak' of the cut, to be free of the encumbrance. I've never been one for jewellery.

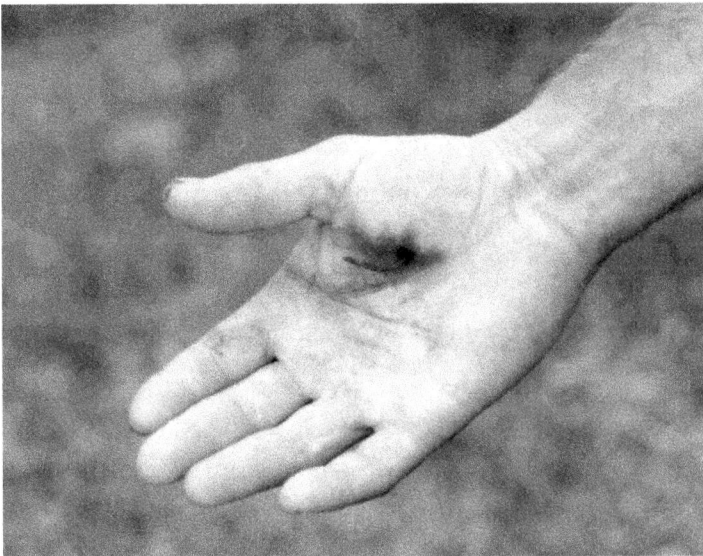

Above: *The 'hook in hand' saga. (Photo courtesy of Mike Thom.)*

I immediately went back to spinning, but the twang of the line on the piece of hook which still protruded from my hand was intolerably uncomfortable and the ache was increasing, so fairly soon I packed it in. We returned to camp and Mike offered to drive me the two or three kilometres (but twenty minute drive!) to Zithulele, a mission hospital that served that isolated and remote area. The foreign doctor looked a little taken aback at my predicament. I in turn looked at his blood-smeared and stained white coat and wondered at his own predicament. He eyed me and grinned.

"Ziss can be kvite deeficoolt, zair har nerfs hent tendonz in za vay. Ze hook must come howt backvoortz, or za nerfs hent tendonz may be damooched. Hi vil inshect viss local henisthetic. Hoh K?"

It was better than OK. It was a damn good thing he was available and willing to help a careless fisherman despite obviously being extremely busy with far more serious cases. Judging by the volume of local anaesthetic he pumped in, he either had a naturally generous nature or he anticipated it was going to be extremely painful. After allowing an appropriate time for the anaesthetic to work and for me to recover from its application, he prepared me for the next bit.

"Ziss vil nhot be heezy. Hi kennot poosh ze hook sroo forevoorts, hit must come howt backvoortz. Hit vil take mush heffort...errrr...fors, to pool aghenst za bahb orf za hook, hew know?" He grinned again, which was encouraging. He was right on all counts: the strength of

190

human tissue is remarkable and it took very considerable effort on his part. With large surgical pliers he manoeuvred and persevered and eventually wrenched the hook out backwards, against the barb. He daubed some mercurochrome or similar disinfectant over the hole and protruding bits, and assured me it should be fine. I was enormously grateful and thanked him profusely.

Off we went and by evening I was fishing again. I had no further problem with it.

While fishing on Table Rock one night I had my third (and hopefully last) close encounter with the sea. Considering the depth of the sea around Table Rock, it was normally a surprisingly dry spot to fish from, even in moderately heavy swells. Nevertheless, no matter how safe a spot seems or is reputed to be, one can simply never drop one's guard.

Above: *The author, squandering his life away on Table Rock in pursuit of big fish. Note the concrete access bridge (and escape route) on the left of the rock. (Photo courtesy of Mike Thom.)*

Anyone fishing Table Rock owes a considerable debt of gratitude to whoever went to the trouble of building a concrete access bridge. At high tide big swells lift huge volumes of water up and over the lower rocks surrounding the table. These swells often absolutely roar past behind the table, under the bridge and down through large cracks and crevices back into the sea. However only in enormous seas at high tide would the big rock at the start of the bridge (on the left in the photograph) cop a deluge. This was extremely rare, and getting on top of the rock or behind it afforded good protection in emergencies.

In rough weather, if one were unfortunate enough to fall into a large wave's flow of water under the bridge and be washed into the deep gully on the left, one would be lucky to suffer only injury. In the daytime that is; at night time to get out alive would take a miracle.

On the night in question the sea was somewhat unsettled. The occasional big swell was rolling in and rushing past with its usual bluster, looking far more threatening than it would eventually turn out to be. Overall though, the sea had a certain feel of unpredictability about it, and I must admit to feeling a little ill at ease. It wasn't peaceful fishing. There was some sort of a moon, but as usual I was also depending on my miner's headlamp to detect approaching swells well enough in advance to get out of their way. This entailed a quick dash back across the bridge to the safety of the high rock behind the table, while releasing the necessary fishing line and keeping enough tension on this to keep it off the rocks.

The trick lay in guessing which swell threatened trouble and which would pass by harmlessly, as did the vast majority. During the course of the evening's fishing I had made a number of dashes, all unnecessary, for the sanctuary of the big rock. Every time the water roared harmlessly under the bridge. On the final occasion, for some unknown reason instead of going all the way back to the rock which I had already done many times, I decided just to stop in the middle of the concrete bridge and wait while the water passed underneath. The wave which persuaded me to take that precautionary step was nothing out of the ordinary. It appeared no different, no bigger or more threatening than any of its predecessors from which I had taken the usual refuge.

I moved back to the centre of the bridge, stopped, steadied myself and checked my line. Then I watched for what I could make out of the swell's progress in the dull moonlight and beam of my headlamp. Still nothing unusual. Nothing unusual that is, until it hit something somewhere in a way or at an angle that none of the others had done. CRASH! I watched transfixed as a mass of white sea water climbed in front of me. There was no time to turn and run – I barely had time to check my footing. The wide column of water climbed and spread as I stood there. Most fortunately it fragmented progressively into dense heavy spray rather than remaining solid water. I knew I was in for trouble, but there was nothing I could do. The water climbed, slowed and started falling towards me. I braced for the deluge and down it came. Even though it had turned into spray, its downward force was so strong that I had to push upwards against it to stop myself from collapsing, but the total saving grace was that it came down so close to vertical that it didn't push me backwards off the bridge. That would have been disastrous.

As the deluge passed and water poured off me, I became acutely aware that I was OK and that I had had an incredibly close shave. The relief was massive, but I was still close to crapping myself. Both feelings lasted for some time. I reeled in, packed my gear and got my butt out of there, not even wanting to look back.

My close (sometimes *uncomfortably* close) association with the sea, not least of all this last experience, has led me to one unshakeable conclusion – the only thing that is totally predictable about the sea is that it is ultimately *un*predictable. Better to regard it as such.

One of the most exciting aspects of Mbolompo and surrounds was the capacity of the area to deliver the unexpected. Potential fish variety was enormous. In addition to the common species already mentioned, tuna, kingfish, bonito, pompano (*Trachinotus blochii*), silver bream (*Rhabdosargus sarba* – my biggest weighed 15 lb) and musselcracker could also be encountered there, albeit only very rarely in some cases.

*Left: A 15 lb silver bream or stumpnose (*Rhabdosargus sarba) *caught on crayfish bait at Mbolompo in 1978.*

The last fishing story for the area offers another example of both the size and variety of fish available there. It was early evening, and dark except for a quarter or so moon. I had moved to Table Rock, away from two companions who preferred to stay at nearby East Wind Bay on the opposite side of the point. Hooking a kob on pillie, I landed it far up the sheltered gully on the left of Table Rock. I had never had to do this before, not even in daylight. I did so only after shouts for a gaff proved unproductive – though not for lack of volume, mind you. They probably thought the flecks of saliva were light rain. The next pillie attracted an even stronger quarry and shouts for a gaff increased to screams, though still in vain. This time they probably chatted between themselves about how fortunate it was that they didn't have to cast against the howling gale. Pity about the increasing rain though...

Again, after considerable effort to subdue it, the fish had to be manoeuvred right up the gully and over the rocks in its narrows before it could be reached by hand. This time it was a pignose grunter. Both fish weighed 20 lb. After that it was quiet, and we all returned to camp.

The following day I went out in the early morning darkness alone and landed two kob on spoon in East Wind Bay. In the first light I was delighted to land a small shad of perhaps three quarters of a pound. For some reason that morning I felt absolutely certain I was going to catch a poensie; the feeling was uncanny, as though I just couldn't miss.

The shad was delivered with great care to a safe rock pool, and I moved my equipment a short distance to fish from Table Rock. Out went the shad with a faultless cast, and I settled back to enjoy the epitome of a perfect early fishing morning: calm sea, windless, cloudless, sunny and warm. I didn't have too long to enjoy it before the live-bait took off, bumping and jerking in tell-tale fashion – definitely not going for a wander of its own accord. After the standard wait, strike, pump and wind, I found myself on the winning end, but simply unable no matter what I tried, to persuade the fish to move to the left past Table Rock and into the sheltered gaffing gully. Not that there was anybody there to gaff for me; there wasn't, but at least it would have been easier to land there.

With the fish tiring and moving ever closer to the rocks I suddenly found myself with no option but to move down to the rock ledge in front of me and try to lift it into the deep pool at the water's edge using a swell. This pool was only a metre or so above the sea at the time and even small swells were washing in and out of it, though not dangerously so. The water in the pool was well over 1.8 metres deep, and I would still have a problem getting the fish out of that before a swell came along and washed it back into the sea. Once at the sea's edge – which also tells just how very calm it was at the time – I hauled the fish to the surface and confirmed what I had expected: a poensie. With the next swell I lifted it over the edge, from the open sea into the pool.

What next? I couldn't reach to get a grip on the fish and I was grimly determined it wasn't going back out again. What made me decide to actually jump into the pool, rod 'n all, I don't know; presumably perceived necessity and blind resolve. Anyway, I did. Having the rod would at least maintain the connection between fish and me if things went wrong and I couldn't hold it. Admittedly it would under those circumstances be a fragile connection, but better than none. I could always let go of the rod if sufficiently pressed, for example to avoid drowning or getting washed out into the sea.

As soon as I could after jumping in, I grabbed the barely moving fish through the bottom of its gill and trod water, looking for the way out. I was about to negotiate the side of the pool when I heard a Xhosa voice above me and a hand reached out to grab first the fish, then my rod and then my hand. This was indeed a man who had his priorities right! I had been totally unaware of his arrival.

After helping me out and securing the fish safely in a pool, my benefactor attempted to converse with me. Alas, with my knowledge of Xhosa being as sparse as it was, all I understood of his efforts was his broad grin, which of course is a universal language. What I did know is that I planned to give him something to express my gratitude. I also knew that he was a fisherman himself – I had seen him many times. His reel was badly aged to say the least, and his line consisted of varying breaking strains and colours joined with big knots at uncomfortably close intervals. The line must have been hell to cast with.

We returned to camp and weighed the fish. The poensie weighed 31 lb and the two kob weighed 20 and 12 lb respectively. I dug out a Penn 49 fully loaded with 40 lb line, and presented it to my benefactor with some other items of tackle. Well, if his earlier grin was universal, it now extended into something which was reminiscent of the light from one of the universes' larger suns. His white teeth shone; his delight was a pleasure to behold. We were both very happy chaps!

Not quite so full of smiles were my mates (who had chosen to sleep in) when they saw the morning's catch.

Above, from left to right: *The evening and morning's catch: Two kob of 20 lb each and one of 12 lb, a 31 lb poensie and a 20 lb pignose grunter. The fellow who helped me is standing to my immediate right, holding the poensie which he helped to land. Mbolompo Point and Table Rock are directly behind his head. Note the fairly big swell running.*

At the conclusion of a fishing trip, every time I drove out of the mountains and valleys leading down to the magical Mbolompo, I would feel a great sense of loss. I would wonder to myself whether somehow this might be my last trip. I always hated leaving. This did ultimately happen the year before I left for Australia, but fortunately at the time I didn't know that or I might not have been prepared to drive up those rugged tracks leading through the hills and out of the place I loved so much.

* * *

When an old South African friend recently heard I was writing my fishing memoirs, he asked if I was planning to include our ski-boat fishing escapades in the story, and did I remember how sea-sick I used to get. HELL! Did I remember? I would hurl with such force that the stuff would shoot out in a jet without touching my teeth. If you exhumed my body a thousand years from now and created a new me from the bits, *that* memory would still be alive and well, if nothing else.

"Nope, doesn't ring a bell. Whatcha talkin' about?"

I tried to deny the fact that the escapades had ever taken place. After all it could look a bit embarrassing considering my earlier less-than-complimentary comments about the boatie-brigade – though I must say, the often dangerous game of South African ski-boat fishing was not what I had in mind when I down-played boat fishing. My denials produced a sympathetic cluck-clucking, and something about the tragedy of Alzheimer's striking ever younger people.

The questioner, Pieter Nel, was a friend with whom I had fished many times on his ski-boat out of the Kaaiman's River mouth, north of George in the Cape Province. Memories of sea-sickness pushed Alzheimer's out of the way and I recalled some interesting events on those wonderful trips. The place we launched from was scenically beautiful, but a pig of a place to launch from: a narrow bay lying between two stretches of rather rugged and toothy rocks.

To add to this, the only access to it was via a tidal river, and one could only travel down the river and launch the boat on a reasonably high tide. To add to *this*, when it snowed on the Outeniqua mountain range, the snow-melt chose the Kaaiman's river for its passage to the sea. This occurred mainly when we were trying to negotiate the kilometre or so of shallow water between the boat ramp and the sea, jumping out and pushing the boat wherever there was insufficient depth to use the motors. And that was almost everywhere. Well, that's what my now improving memory recalls quite vividly anyway.

Icy water would reach the body's most sensitive parts, when in the dark (yes, we were often there in the dark when the tide required it) we would step into a hole or over a sandy drop-off into the depths, clutching the boat for support and straining to keep as much of the body above water as possible. Of course the deep water never lasted long enough to allow us to jump on board and motor our way for more than a few metres.

All too often we would push and heave our way right down to the sea, only to find as day dawned that the sea was far too rough to launch. By then the tide would have dropped so low that to get back to the boat ramp we would sometimes even have to take the two motors off and carry them a distance, then return to push the now light*er* (but not light) boat back as well. Heave bloody ho! Yes, thank you Piet, it's all coming back now, with amazing clarity.

But I loved it all the same. Who wouldn't? It was adventure after all. Like the occasion I had run out of bad language by the time we reached the sea, but it was so beautifully calm, windless and cloudless that we both rapidly recovered our composure and prepared to set off. I took my place at the back of the boat...

Let me explain for the benefit of Aussie readers that in South Africa, a ski-boat (why that particular name I wouldn't have a clue) is a small but seaworthy recreational fishing boat fitted with two outboard motors, usually equal in size and referred to as 'twins'. Having two substantial motors is a clever idea of the South Africans who through bitter experience have discovered that if you only have one motor, and this packs up (as outboards do from time to time) and the wind happens to be blowing out to sea (as it always is when a motor packs up), you don't just wash up safely on the beach and live happily ever after. The remarkable number of small-craft sea rescues in Australia shows quite clearly that Aussies have not cottoned onto this yet. Instead you have to carry hundreds of dollars worth of safety gear and satellite beacons, because sooner or later, with only one motor, you are bound to get into trouble. Hello-oo…hello-oo…

Anyway, on this beautiful calm crisp day, as soon as the warmth of the early morning sun had defrosted our bodily extremities, I was ready to roll, seated at the stern, facing backwards towards the two motors. This was for restarting and other emergencies should we hit sand and have a motor cut out – not good when launching through the surf. No electric-start luxuries for us in those days. Naturally, the waves had grown by the time Piet hit the throttles, and just as naturally, they would die down again as soon as we were through, when it didn't matter any more – a phenomenon definitely also linked to King Neptune's thought processes.

I wasn't concerned. Not only was Piet a very capable surf navigator; he was also cautious. I was unfazed as we crashed through the waves one by one, Piet throttling back or giving it stick as required, always keeping the bow well and truly into the swells or broken waves as we proceeded. Suddenly, as was not uncommon, we hit sand. Seconds later we were free again and Piet hit the power to get ahead to beat a breaking wave. But shit! Only half of what should have happened did happen, and instantly we realized we had lost power from one outboard, despite the fact that it was still running.

THE LOST PROP DEBACLE

While Piet manoeuvred, I lifted the still running motor to see what was wrong. Well, you could have gunned that motor till you were blue in the face and nothing would have happened. The propeller was gone.

With one motor out we simply didn't have the power to risk turning round between waves – we had no option but to press on until we were clear of the surf. And this we did, not easily or comfortably, but we did. When this had been achieved, Piet made the unhappy but absolutely right decision. On that beautiful morning, when we had just got through the nasty bit, he turned us around, positioned us between two unbroken swells and headed back for shore, gunning what was left of our power to the max. Both swells eventually broke with a crash, one in front, one behind, as Piet battled to keep us ahead of the latter's threatening wall of white water.

The waves diminished to a low whisper as we beached with a sigh of relief. However, the sigh of relief transformed without a break to a sigh of resignation as soon as we saw our new predicament: a dropping tide and a hell of a long wait until the next high tide if we didn't move our butts and get the boat up the river, pronto! My memory tells me that this was one of the mornings when the motors had to be taken off and portaged – if that's the right term – whatever term means *they didn't carry themselves* is the right one. Sheesh kebab, the things we did for fun.

The things we did for fun? That immediately reminds me of the anchor episode. We were several kilometres out from land on a choppy sea, both outboards purring, but with the anchor stuck on a rocky bottom. No amount of manual encouragement (which was my job as the crew of one) made one iota of difference to the anchor on its hundred or so feet of now vertical rope. We would have to pull the thing inside-out to get it off, which meant fastening the rope and gunning the motors. So Piet said, "Wind it up and hold on tight."

I did the former admirably and the latter rather poorly. If only we had had a video camera, we would have walked off with a 'Funniest Home Videos' prize for sure. The boat surged forward, rapidly taking up the rope's slack as we sped ahead. I clung to the coils of rope, ready to release them should the need arise. Well, it was yours truly who got released rather than the rope – with a vengeance. As the rope's slack came to an end and it tightened suddenly, the boat swerved hard to the side. I on the other hand carried on straight, but in a somersault the likes of which I could not have performed to order had I practised it for months.

I hit the water, arms and legs flailing. This was an 'Oh, what a feeling!' of the absolutely crappiest kind, and instinctively and instantly I began working on my salvation by simultaneously trying to touch bottom and walk on top of the water. No reasonable request from the mind to the body could be rejected under the circumstances, even though the water was close to a hundred feet deep. Then to add to my woes, a sudden internal pressure developing around my posterior parts awoke me to a new threat – crapping myself and the danger of sharks being attracted by my bodily wastes.

At last Piet pulled up next to me – laughing. The way I saw it, seeing as my current predicament was no laughing matter, he must obviously have been laughing at some incredibly funny thing I had said earlier. I normally appreciate people enjoying my humour, as it happens so rarely, but this was a very inappropriate time to be doing so. He managed to stop laughing long enough to pull me in and we managed to free the anchor. I don't remember if we caught any fish that day.

PS. Upon reflection now, many years later and after frequent unavoidable exposures to my own bodily evacuations, I realize with certainty that my concerns at the time over accidental faecal release were unfounded – any sharks within miles would have been violently repelled.

So, those are a few of the recollections of my ski-boating days. Pardon? Ah yes, the fish. Yes, well, I can't really talk about those can I – as I said, it's a bit embarrassing after my anti-boat comments, though there was the 50 lb red steenbras (*Petrus rupestris*) that I caught on a hand-line off the Wilderness, but that was easy 'cos it was caught from a boat, you know. I still have several scars on my hands to prove just how easy it was…

Naaah, to talk about the fish we caught would be hypocritical – ask Piet. He'll tell you how ridiculously easy it is to catch fish from a boat. Just don't ask him about the even bigger red steenbras he lost on the same day when his line broke after a gargantuan battle, or you might get the wrong impression. My ears also bear scars from the bad language that issued forth that day from his normally gentlemanly lips.

Let me finish on a more truthful note, difficult as that might be. Those ski-boating days were fun, exciting and hair-raising; but nothing, not even the vomiting, remains as strongly etched in my memory as the mystery of dropping a big bait onto those deep reefs and wondering what might grab it – and plenty did. Thanks for the memories Piet, seriously this time.

Part Two: Australia

Chapter 8

Ingham and Dungeness Creek, North Queensland: Encounters With Barra, a Sea Snake, Monster Mullet, and Other Amazing Fishing in Two Tiny Back-Waters

The move to Australia had some startling moments in its early days. My family and I arrived in the middle of a severe drought, a few days before Christmas of 1990. We moved into a house on a beautiful piece of land amongst rainforest up in the hills outside Ingham in North Queensland. Within a week of our arrival the drought broke, or rather it was annihilated, smashed to smithereens. Over one night alone we measured 300 mm of rain, though that was not all that fell by any means. Welcome to Australia! Mind you, it wasn't *totally* typical – there was no bush fire threatening the house beforehand.

Vast areas of sugarcane were left under water and we were completely cut off from civilization. We were yet to learn that the rest of Australia would have regarded this as a contradiction in terms. No, not being cut off, but the idea that there is civilization in Queensland. But we were new and this flooding meant a possible lack of food - though not water of course. There was certainly no risk of dehydration. As it turned out the water subsided and we didn't starve. Furthermore, when we were at last able to get into the town of Ingham, I learned of a most interesting aspect of the flood. It was very important to the reproductive cycle of the legendary barramundi (*Lates calcarifer*). What could be more important than that? Ever since making this discovery, I have been in favour of floods.

Shortly after arriving in Ingham (though not within *seconds* as I was now a family man) I went on my traditional 'voyage of discovery' in search of fishable waters. I travelled far and wide, but this proved not to be the home of wild water beating against high cliffs. It was more a matter of almost moribund, often dirty water, on the inside of the great barrier reef, lapping gently (on a rough day) on miles of muddy beaches.

Had I wanted to, I could have caught plenty of sharks, rays and shovelnoses, but as always I was interested in edibles. Realising that I would have to make do with whatever venues were available, I turned my attention to convenience rather than magnificence. Once again the gods of fishing decided to exercise compassion and guide me in my search.

On my travels I discovered a most remarkable little body of water. That is to say, on *average* it was a little body of water. At big high tides it had a modest amount of water; at big lows it was almost waterless – literally. This phenomenon was Dungeness Creek, encountered on the road to Lucinda, near Ingham. What it lacked in magnitude and magnificence it more than made up for in fascination and reliable deliveries of very acceptable fish. It was hard to believe that such an unimpressive location so close to civilization could harbour so many fish, and for that matter, so much marine life in general. This seems to be characteristic of North Queensland, or at least parts of it.

Above: *Dead calm at high tide, before the run-out.*

I visited Dungeness Creek as often as possible during my 18 month stay in the area. Most productive times proved to be approximately 10.00 pm to 2.00 am. On no occasion did I ever fish Dungeness in the daylight, and have no idea how it might have fished then. Nor did I ever encounter anyone else fishing it during the hours that I did. I was always on my own. Although some fish were caught on a rising tide, the best results occurred at the turn of a high tide, and for some time after the run-out commenced. Then all would go quiet. The variety and number of marine animals never ceased to amaze me. Barramundi were top of the angling list, but mangrove jack (rock salmon to South Africans) and rock cod were also quite frequent captures.

Live mullet were the bait of choice, and these were caught in another interesting area of water: the Anabranch, an anabranch connecting two parts of the Herbert River. On moonless nights mullet would usually be thick and there would be no difficulty in catching them. About fifteen mullet of 13 to 15 cm were the maximum that could be safely carried to Dungeness in a twenty litre bucket without losing them through lack of oxygen. Upon arrival at Dungeness they were kept in a bucket with a perforated lid, floating on the end of a rope. Luckily no crocs ever discovered these or me, although there were signs in place to warn of their possible presence.

I recall a hunt for bait one dark night during an exceptionally high tide at the Anabranch. There were extensive shallows in these circumstances, and when mullet were plentiful the sweep of a torch beam would cause a wave of reaction. The surface would erupt in a roar of jumping, flopping, flurrying fish. I had netted the area often enough to be aware, even in the dark, where the channels were. These not large, and even they would be virtually empty at low tide. Nevertheless it paid to target them if possible in the hope of netting larger bait and avoiding the multitudes of smaller ones massed in the shallower water. Extracting and releasing large numbers of undersized fish is difficult and time-consuming enough in the daylight. It can be a major undertaking in the dark.

On this particular night as usual I aimed for the channels in the hope of getting larger fish. The higher powers that control such things must have sensed my silent request. All of these powers put their heads together, and when my net landed I thought the world was coming to an end, or that at the very least I'd made my first close acquaintance with a crocodile. The water under the net erupted with a roar. I fumbled for my head-lamp switch to see whether I should negotiate or run.

To my relief the light beam produced multiple flashes of silver which immediately showed the cause to be fish and not something more sinister. These were protesting with violent indignation, which I guess was not unreasonable under the circumstances. I dragged the heavy thrashing net through the shallow water trying to find a place where I could examine the catch without getting half drowned in the process. When I eventually did manage to release them, in addition to the many usable bait-size mullet were five monsters, the largest of which could not have been less than three pounds. I couldn't believe that such big fish would be present in such a small body of water. They must have been having a close conference for me to get so many at once. I carried them individually, still kicking like mad, back to deep enough water to accommodate them upright, then looked skywards and addressed the higher powers.

"Are you kidding? Come on guys, I'm fishing for barra, not bloody marlin. I won't ask next time – I'll just take pot luck."

Amongst the other species that would turn up from time to time with the mullet was a brackish water fish quite well known in the aquarium trade: 'scats' (*Scatophagus argus*). I only came across smallish specimens of 4 to 6 cm. It was fascinating to capture what I had always regarded as a rather exotic fish, but this is typical of Australia with its abundance of beautiful and well known aquarium species such as archer fish (*Toxites jaculatrix*) which are frequently encountered in the wild. Fortunately conservation laws have protected these to the extent that many are still plentiful.

The scats would register their objection to the cast net in a strange sort of way. They would do everything they could to extend their stay. This was achieved by opening up their fin spines to the greatest possible extent, and holding them there. Despite a 'non-slip' sand-papery skin texture which made them easier to handle, they could be quite difficult to untangle. To add to this problem, their spines are poisonous and produce quite a nasty sting if they end up in the wrong spot – which they did manage occasionally with me, though I never received anything more serious than a simple warning shot.

For several reasons I was occasionally short of live mullet bait. On an active night's fishing things could be pretty brisk, and the mullet could all be used up. It was also invariably much more difficult to find mullet on moonlit nights than dark ones, even at the Anabranch. On such brisk nights if I ran out, or if the Anabranch was not in a generous mood, in desperation I would sometimes try to net them around Dungeness Creek itself. This involved throwing the cast net virtually blindly into occasional small open areas amongst the dense mangroves. These openings had to be detected as well as could be managed in the dark, because a torch light would scare the mullet away. Over time I came to realize quite conclusively that the reason for the lack of mangroves in these little openings is that mangroves don't grow on rocks and that rocks were inevitably to be found where mangroves weren't.

Throwing a monofilament cast net into these openings was like playing that game where paper covers rock, scissors cut paper, rock buggers up scissors etc. There were only two variations in this version. Net covers rock, rock destroys net. It was not a happy mix and my monofil net suffered considerable damage. Wading into these waters at night to free the net was also not a pleasure, but cast nets, like a few other things, do not grow on trees.

One night while throwing a net for mullet in this net-unfriendly area, I made a surprise acquaintance with a hitherto unmet member of the local fauna. At first I had that sense of great victory and doubtless a smug smile to match, when I felt a promising weight in the net. What was even more promising is that the net and its weight continued to move towards me as I pulled. Not rock this time – YA LITTLE BEE-YOODY! I had learned to speak quite sophisticated Australian by then. However, upon lifting the net all sense of victory and smug smile left me like rats deserting a sinking ship. No mullet here, but WHAT

THE...? Had I been wearing false teeth, I would most definitely have ended up grovelling for *them* amongst the rocks. Hell, I nearly lost my *real* ones. I was totally aghast to lift the net and find a large sea snake in it.

I was familiar with their existence and poisonous bite but had never seen one, and sure as hell wasn't expecting one here. Welcome to Australia's wildlife! This fellow turned out to be remarkably docile, and during the time it took to extract it from the net and release it, the snake showed not the slightest sign of aggression. I think I might even have seen it smile, but decided against a Rex Hunt-style farewell kiss on those serpentine lips before returning it unceremoniously whence it came.

Another unwelcome catch in the area was enormous eels with matching teeth, at least 1.5 metres in length, caught on live-baits commissioned for better things. They were not as docile as the sea snake – by a dangerous margin – and I made sure I stayed well clear of their chompers which were *very* impressive. They too did not receive any Rex Hunt brand of affectionate farewell. I valued my face too much.

On the welcome side from the creek was a good supply of barramundi, the biggest about 12 lb, followed by mangrove jack up to about 6 lb and a few estuary cod, also up to 6 lb. A few barra were caught on lures in the pitch dark, but most were caught on live mullet.

Above: *Some Dungeness barramundi and mangrove jack.*

The sudden loud smack of a barra hunting its prey at the surface close by in the silent darkness of the very early hours of morning made a mighty strong impact – similar in magnitude, if not actual sound, to one's trousers tearing when bending over too far. It grabbed one's attention in no uncertain terms.

These surface gulpings of barra were often successfully used in the darkness as a guide to the fishes' whereabouts. A live mullet without a sinker, and hooked through the upper jaw, sometimes with a small float to keep it near the surface, would be allowed to drift in the direction of the sound, using the flow of the water. There can be few better means for keeping one's adrenalin-pumping system in top physical shape than releasing a live mullet bait into swirling black water in the pitch dark, and waiting with fingers primed on a free-running spool, in anticipation of a strike.

Waiting…waiting…waiting…whack, smash and run! Or on occasion, more challengingly, it would be tug – tug, a few jerks and a tentative run. Or damnably disappointingly, the fish would feel the hook and just *drop* the bait……. *SHII-IIT! How annoying is that?* A positive strike would often be followed by an eruption somewhere out there in the darkness as the surprised fish detected the hook and registered its objection to the Trojan mullet's barbed inner occupant by jumping and shaking its head violently. All too often bait, hook and fish would part company and take off in different directions, the resultant slack line instantly producing a state of disbelief followed by mental replays:

"What if I had struck sooner, harder, later, not so hard, not at all, twice, three times…?"

"Forget it mate, it's gawn."

"Who said that?"

"The bringer of bad tidings, hard facts and bitter truth."

"Piss off! What if I had struck sooner, harder, later, not so hard, not at all, twice, three times…?"

"Forget it mate, let it go…"

If the hooks stayed put, then hard runs punctuated by occasional jumps could be expected until the fish was subdued. Leaping from the water would sometimes be reserved until they sensed land approaching without their approval, but once tired, unlike the dogged fight-to-the-end mentality of mangrove jack and trevally, they would often throw in the towel and allow themselves to be brought to the edge with little further ado.

After losing a number of fish to lines cut by their extremely sharp gill covers, I opted to use a short nylon-covered steel trace of just 12 to 15 cm. This would sometimes be sensed and result in a dropped bait, but no more fish were lost due to cut lines.

Mangrove jack and cod were caught on bottom live-baits. Mangrove jack would scream off at a tremendous rate, and continue fighting until they were beached. If anything they were better eating than barramundi too. The cod were less than impressive in the fighting department, but made up for this once they appeared on the menu. In their case, quite frequently by the time the strike was made, the hook and bait would already have been subjected to their digestive juices, so deep would they have been swallowed. Their presence on the line was sometimes only detected when a bait was retrieved to check its condition – which in the event of having been swallowed by a cod would be rather poor.

As mentioned, there were signs warning of the risk of encountering crocodiles, but I never met any there, or anywhere else for that matter other than a zoo. However I did encounter a large nest of small 'wild' bees or wasps under a railway bridge while fishing in the area one night. I don't know what kind they were or anything else about them but they were fierce defenders of their nest and they stung like hell. I felt that I didn't really need to know any more about the little devils though I did learn something about myself. I learned how fast I could run along a railway bridge in the dark without falling and breaking my neck, when necessity demanded.

Another interesting phenomenon for a new arrival in Australia was the large groups of fruit bats or flying foxes socializing in nearby trees. The most impressive thing about them was the *racket* they made. Crikey, could they party – obviously an Aussie thing. Now that I come to think of it, those things, along with *clouds* of mozzies and *swarms* of sandflies, meant that Dungeness was not always a peaceful or comfortable place to fish. But it was beautiful, mysterious, fascinating and rewarding, and I loved it – good, bad, bites, and all!

It was in Ingham that my two sons decided to follow the family tradition.

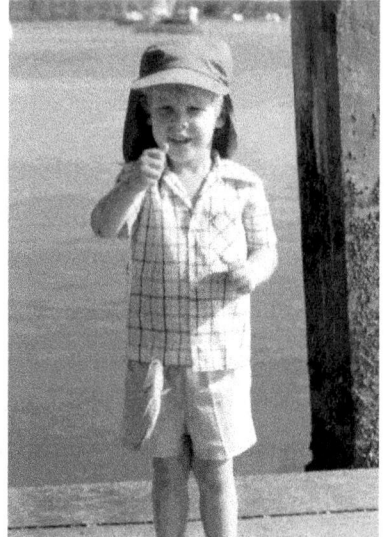

Above: *The author's sons, Ken (left) and Chris, with their first fish catches, from the jetty at Lucinda, North Queensland.*

Above: *Chris and Ken a few years later – scaling up in New South Wales.*

Chapter 9

Brisbane – Noosa's Hell's Gates: Happy Moments (Not!), Butter Bream, and Big Fish in Difficult Water

The Ingham period ended with a move to Brisbane. Although a city was not first on my list of top sites to live, maps indicated that the coastline to the north boasted a useful amount of promising looking coastal rock. Furthermore, there was no barrier to the oceanic swells that form such an important part of decent rock fishing.

Naturally, a recce trip was needed. The rock started at Caloundra, and although this area yielded my one and only golden trevally (*Gnathanodon speciosus*) to date, weighing

11 lb, I generally baulk at the idea of fishing anywhere within sight of a house, let alone city lights, so trips here were rare.

Above: *11 lb golden trevally caught at Caloundra on a whole pilchard.*

My search took me further and further afield, all along the Sunshine Coast until at last I reached a truly magical place. (Why couldn't I have fished this area a hundred years ago, with today's tackle of course?) This magnificent rocky headland, although quite near to civilization, was in a national park and situated such that it felt as though it was miles from anywhere. The parkland was the beautiful coastal reserve at Noosa. More specifically, I had discovered Hell's Gates, an enormously impressive spot at the end of a long stretch of fishable rocks, all dropping into tantalizingly deep and fishy looking water.

Most unfortunately, Hell's Gates turned out to be better to look at than to fish from – though not due to any shortage of fish. I also discovered that the place had been well named. The most hellish part was the walk there carrying a swag of fishing gear, and then back again after a night's fishing, especially if a decent fish had been caught. A second very problematic aspect of the place was the difficulty it presented in getting a large fish out – difficult in the day, hellish at night.

Yet another negative was the difficulty in catching good live-bait in the daytime, in preparation for a night's fishing. One reason for this was the almost inevitable presence of the fish called 'Happy Moments' (*Siganus spinus*) in plague proportions.

Up until the time I discovered 'Happy Moments' I was quite content to use the South African Hottentot fish (whose strange name is referred to earlier in the book) to epitomise the quaintness of some fish names. In this respect, Hottentots were dropped like hot bricks in favour of Happy Moments on the day that I personally experienced the 'reasoning' behind the name. In any other country in the world one would expect the name to have come about thanks to some especially delightful facet of the fish – beautiful colour, good tucker, great live-bait etc. Yeah right! In this case, rather than that, the name is a prize example of

Australia's twisted, tongue-in-cheek brand of humour. Not surprisingly, it makes *me* feel right at home!

The fish are so named because they are blessed with the ability to sting. Not the sort of sensation that leaves the question in one's mind, "Am I just being a wuss?" (Wuss = sissy to South African readers) No. This is a break-out-in-a-cold-sweat magnitude of pain, more like, "Oh no! Will I have to abandon fishing and head home to see a vet – NOW?" And consequently, they are called 'Happy Moments'. Yeah, I can see the logic in that, couldn't have come up with a better name myself...

My first such deliriously happy experience occurred when I had caught my umpteenth specimen while desperately looking for a decent live-bait – which they categorically are *not*. It seems beneath the dignity of any marine creature to consume them – though some people apparently do. The latter is hearsay as I have not personally witnessed this phenomenon.

As I was removing the tiny hook, the fish flicked free and a dorsal spine entered one side of that thin section of skin between the middle and fore finger of my hand (the web in a frog or duck), and exited the other side – straight through. I was quite used to body punctures of this nature from fish, and muttered something along the lines of "Oops" or "Gosh" – or something like that – while extracting it. I then continued removing the hook from the fish with a little more care. Seconds later I raised an eyebrow. This puncture was not behaving normally. A few minutes later I knew I was in trouble. Not too long *there*after I was saying, "Oh-

ohhh, how much worse is this going to get?" Well, as a matter of fact it got quite a lot worse before the intensely aching sting stabilized at a level which was just bearable enough for me to hang in and ride it out. It was probably some thirty minutes before the pain subsided to a level at which fishing activities could be resumed at a tolerable level of discomfort.

Nowadays I handle Happy Moments with very great care and have no hesitation in suggesting to everyone except my worst enemies that they do the same. Happy bloody Moments indeed!

Two more fortuitous discoveries eventually enabled me to land a total of four jewfish (kob, *Argyrosomus hololepidotus*) just to the left of Hell's Gates, before deciding after eight or nine trips in all, that the extreme difficulty in landing a decent fish at night from those rocks made fishing the area simply not worthwhile. The four landed fish weighed between 26 and 31 lb. The discoveries that led to them were firstly that jewfish were *very* partial to butter bream (*Monodactylus argenteus*) presented as a live-bait, and secondly that these were almost as plentiful and easy to catch at night as Happy Moments were in the day. And they don't sting!

Above and right: *Two kob from Hell's Gates, 29 and 31lb, caught at night on live butter bream. Note the bundle of long rods, and bamboo gaff pole whose hook so frequently interrupted the walk on the path through the bushes. ("Damn – hooked on a bloody tree again!")*

The jewfish could be expected, with remarkable reliability, to become active any time between 10.00 pm and 2.00 am; sometimes later, occasionally earlier. I lost far more big fish than I caught, usually while trying to land them, which was extremely tricky especially when I was fishing on my own. These were frequently lost at the surface after positive identification. It is certainly a 'fishy' area, some of the fish being so large that I had no control over them even when they could be turned and brought to the rocks. They simply travelled left or right where I couldn't follow, or went under the ledges and cut the 50 lb line. This was exciting but frustrating fishing. What the very big fellows were I have no idea, possibly big cod, maybe very big jewfish. Their behaviour was neither ray nor shark-like. The latter however were certainly present, the larger specimens of which would head for the horizon unstoppably.

Having discovered how good the butter bream were, I always used them live for bait. They could almost invariably be caught even late at night, on a very small hook with a little piece of pilchard tied on with cotton. As far as live-baits go, they stayed alive well, often for hours. A single 5/0 or 6/0 short shank hook was hooked through the back just in front of the dorsal fin. More than one hook was too easily detected by jewfish, resulting in baits being picked up and dropped almost immediately. Even with one hook they would often drop the bait after a short run – very frustrating. On nights when the fish were active I could have perhaps eight to ten runs in the course of a night, but jewfish in particular could be difficult to hook.

Then, even if there was only a light to moderate sea running, landing the fish at night would be difficult at best and dangerous at worst. A seemingly almost inevitable wash from right to left would easily take a large fish past the only opportunity to get it close enough for landing. This opportunity was via a very small rocky inlet situated to the left of a rock which jutted out a short way from the steeply sloping edge, and extended well out of the water. The jutting rock was a good place from which to gaff in a *very* calm sea at low tide in the daytime.

However, if the sea was anything but exceptionally calm in the daytime, and in any sea at night, the fish had to be negotiated past this protruding rock in the hope that the small inlet could be successfully exploited. If the fish could be brought into the inlet there was a reasonable chance of holding it there long enough to gaff, though passing swells could, and frequently did pull it back out into the sea. If the fish washed back out or past the entrance, both of which happened very easily, it would be lost. There was virtually no chance of pulling a big fish back against the wash – at least I never achieved it. The odds were stacked in the fish's favour. In a sense these difficulties are a pity, as it is no less than magnificent fishing terrain, but at least this means it will probably always be under-fished – unless the boaties discover it of course!

While I have observed game fish in the area, seen a smallish yellow-tail kingfish being lost and know of one being caught (on a butter bream fillet), my only catch in this category was a small bonito on a tin spoon. This fish fought like a far larger fish and I was most surprised at its small size of around three or four pounds. The area oozes potential for perseverance with live-baits on balloons, or similar land-based game fishing techniques. Pity about the long walk.

Chapter 10

Inskip: The Channel Between the Mainland and Fraser Island – Home to Big Critters and Heavy Rain: a Cobia, Giant Herring, and Some *Big* Shovelnoses

Once the decision was made to abandon Hell's Gates in favour of less demanding venues, an alternative had to be found which could deliver the goods. A friend told me about the water between Fraser Island's southern tip and the mainland. His mouth-watering tales of game fish from the beach left me in no doubt that a visit was long overdue.

As I did not have access to a four wheel drive vehicle at this time, my recce trips were restricted to parking where the less fortunate masses park, and foot-slogging my way around. What I found, even with such restricted access, was indeed mouth-watering. This southern oceanic gateway to Hervey Bay is huge; the fact that tuna and dolphin are regular visitors through the waterway is a clear indicator of its size. The speed and volume of the massive tidal flow are awe-inspiring to say the least.

Due to my lack of four wheel drive transport, my first efforts were perforce directed towards the vicinity of the Fraser Island barges' departure point – a kilometre or two inland from the sea. This is seriously deep water which moves rapidly with tidal flow but exhibits relatively little sea swell movement, except during very rough seas on an incoming tide. It is more difficult, in the daytime at least, to induce big fish to take a bait in these calm conditions in clear water. This is partly because foreign objects in the bait such as line, swivels and protruding hooks are so easily visible. Furthermore, by contrast, in a rough turbulent environment prey must be captured as rapidly as possible once detected – that is, grab first, ask questions (or feel hooks) later. There is more time in calm clear water to examine a live-bait which is unnaturally incapacitated and can't get away. Probably at least partly for this reason, the area delivered plenty of tailor, sharks, rays, and some very large shovelnoses, but only one decent sized edible fish – to me at least. However the unusualness of this edible catch, recounted later, was such that it was worth many lesser species of a similar size.

A new venue tends to spur one on. The mystery and anticipation of fishing unknown waters for the first time – especially deep water known to be home to large denizens – would always push me to exercise maximum effort. In this case that meant having two lines out all night. If the body was less resilient than the mind then the rods would be placed in rod holders in the sand with ratchets engaged on a free-running spool. I slept close by, arising occasionally whenever woken by a bulging bladder or other bodily discomfort, to check and replenish baits. At least here I was able to dig out a hole in the sand to match my body shape. Well....to match my body shape very approximately that is, but at least it was more accommodating than rock.

Every now and again alarm clocks of a far more attention-grabbing nature than the body would scream and I would leap out of 'bed' and grab the straining rod and screeching reel and strike as quickly as possible. Or I would disengage the ratchet and allow a live-bait to be taken freely, unless the eater had already experienced the ratchet's 'dentist drill' vibrations down the line and had spat the bait out in disgust – a frustrating and all too common event.

Inevitably being woken by a ratchet, whatever the outcome, would produce sufficient adrenalin to keep me awake in the hope that this was the beginning of a period of feeding action. If it were a once-off, the eyelids would eventually become leaden, any remaining adrenalin would be tapped off via the urinary tract, the mattress would get adjusted by removing a few scoops of sand and I would snooze off to await the next interruption.

If the hook set, the captive could be anything from a 25 cm 'grinner' (of the genus *Trachinocephalus* or *Saurida*) which can swallow remarkably large baits for their size, to something that was so large it would seem not even to realize it was hooked. Some *very* big aquatic critters were encountered there. They would move off unstoppably, at their own pace – sometimes fast, sometimes slowly – in a direction entirely of their own choosing, while I, at the losing end, would do everything possible to turn the tables, or at least minimize loss of line. That simply meant hoping that the line would eventually break as near to the fish as possible. Braking pressure would be increased until the inevitable 'pop' and slackening of the line if the break was underwater, or 'crack' if it broke above. A crack would mean a break near the rod – not good, but fortunately extremely rare.

If the fish could be turned, then an often protracted war of wills would ensue, with give and take on both sides. Then, unless the line subsequently parted due to excessive pressure anyway, the fish would be beached. If not edible, every effort would be made to extract the hook, and failing this the line would be cut as close to the hook as possible and the animal returned whence it came, no doubt thinking unsavoury thoughts about its recent experience and the perpetrator.

An enormous advantage of this venue is the incredible ease with which a fish can be landed compared to a rocky environment. This includes the benefit of not having to put maximum pressure on the fish during the fight, provided there is plenty of line available. It is the optimum safe and easy situation for an unaccompanied angler to land a large fish. Unfortunately, considering the number of hours fished at Inskip, my catches were rather low, with only the one exceptional edible fish.

That catch took place in November 1997. I had my two sons with me, aged nine and eleven. They were being introduced at a young age to the 'no pain, no gain' principle as it applies to fishing. They had no 4x4 vehicle nearby to retire to and knew we were there for the long haul. By 1.00 am it was 'all quiet on the western front' and we had long since resorted to various non-fishing activities to amuse ourselves, while a single line remained baited and in the water – more because this would allow us to truthfully claim to have fished all night than in the real hope of catching anything. We were doing whatever we were doing fifteen or twenty metres away from the rod when, rather amazingly, something large discovered the pilchard bait – a bait which should long since have been destroyed by the myriad diminutive sea creatures that scavenge the sea bed at night.

The ratchet screamed in protest and I leapt in its direction, almost airborne in my haste, grabbing the rod and striking in one movement. The pilchard's sudden strange behaviour and unexpectedly spiky 'body parts' prompted its consumer to take off at top speed in the opposite direction. After another hefty strike or two and disengaging the ratchet, I settled down to get the measure of my adversary – and some adversary it was. I was using a Shimano SpeedMaster, and despite its generous line capacity, the rate at which the line diameter was diminishing was somewhat alarming. The situation clearly required increased pressure to avoid the risk of having the reel stripped.

That just seemed to aggravate the fish which increased its own efforts in response; its powerful run was interspersed with jerking tugging movements, reminiscent of a bull terrier having a tug of war, rather than a steady pull. This vigorous action continued unabated right until beaching – the fish simply would not give up. This is in interesting contrast to most sharks (sharks being rather common at this spot), a useful test being to slacken the line and check the reaction. With few exceptions, sharks, especially small ones, simply stop pulling. Edibles maintain an active fight. A notable exception to this is bigger shovelnoses, (*not* the small ones) whose sustained, powerful and fairly active fight continues to the last. Their strength and in particular their endurance is remarkable; far greater by my reckoning than almost any edibles of equivalent size.

The actual loss of line slowly declined, and eventually recovery commenced, with the powerful runs declining little by little in frequency, strength and distance. I remained reasonably convinced it was an edible, or if not an edible then possibly a shovelnose, but it did seem a little too active for that. Only one way to appease the curiosity – make sure the fish stayed on until it could at least be sighted.

When it was finally sufficiently subdued to bring it within reach of a torch beam, it clearly displayed the shape and finnage of a shark, which caught me totally by surprise. Not only surprised but very disappointed. Only the colour didn't seem right. It took some moments for recognition and realization to hit me. This wasn't a shark, it was a *cobia*. GOOD GRIEF! I DON'T *BELIEEEEVE* IT! A cobia (*Rachycentron canadum*) from Inskip beach; I was incredulous, but there was no doubt about it. No wonder it had fought so hard. With *very* great care I accommodated its final twists, turns and lunges, and finally lifted it by hand safely onto dry sand. What a beauty – a dream catch. That is the beauty and mystery of these deep waters: you just don't know what they might deliver.

Above: *A 22 lb cobia (black kingfish)*
caught from Inskip on pilchard at night.

There was no further action that night but it didn't matter; a new milestone had been reached and I was elated. The fish was photographed early the next morning, then taken home for culinary tests which it passed with flying colours. A beautiful fish all round, and a great pity they are not more easily accessible to land-based anglers.

Above: *A 15 lb giant herring caught at Inskip – released alive after posing briefly*

Another interesting species which this area delivered was a large giant herring (*Elops australis*) which took a small live mullet, just after dark on a mild summer evening in 1998. It put up a good scrap, but uncharacteristically didn't jump even once. At 15 lb this was the largest of the genus I had ever encountered. Unfortunately they are something of a culinary disaster – despite looking so good. Maybe there are recipes which can redeem them, but if there are I am unaware of them, so after obliging me by lying still just long enough for a photograph, this good looking fish was rewarded with its freedom.

A few more excursions to this area delivered mainly small tailor, a plethora of grinners and a goodly number of shovelnoses, including one estimated at over a hundred pounds (see below). I then acquired a Nissan Navara ute (bakkie) whose 4x4 capacity enabled me at last to explore more of this amazing stretch of water. This ute was excellent on the sand. Even with only slightly wider than normal, semi-mud tyres, it never left me stranded.

Above: *A shovelnose estimated at over 100 lb, returned alive after posing. The rod is a heavy 'home-constructed' job, and a veteran of many a fishy altercation involving large adversaries.*

Left: *Another big shovelnose from the Great Sandy Strait area. This one went into the pot (well... several pots), as they are excellent eating.*

As it happens, one of my earliest memories of a trip in this ute relates not to its capacity to negotiate sand, but rather to the astonishing capacity of what should have been a leak-proof canvas canopy, to leak. I have to admit that there may have been some strange poetic justice in this: a sorry story, which I should perhaps recount first to appease my terrible long-standing feelings of guilt.

Some years before on a trip to Mbolompo, I was woken up in the course of the night by a downpour of rain, or more accurately, a bloody deluge. It was accompanied by a howling gale, thunder and lightning. I was most comfortably housed in the totally waterproof fibreglass canopy of my ute. My only concern was how the weather might affect my fishing activities the next morning.

The wind howled and the rain poured so violently that I reluctantly pulled my cosy warm blankets back to look out of the canopy window to see how my two companions might be faring in their tent. They were camped only a few metres away from my vehicle, on a slight slope. What I saw could have come straight out of a cartoon movie. They were *anything* but comfortable. There was a light shining and silhouetted against this, flailing arms, legs and writhing bodies were clearly visible as they attempted to secure their tent and reduce the amount of rain entering it. What they could actually be achieving was a mystery to me, but they were working frantically at it. Certainly their state was anything but one of deep and peaceful sleep. They appeared closer to uprooting the tent and sending it rolling off down the hill into the sea than waterproofing it.

Naturally I instantly leapt out of bed, and without even troubling to don water-proofs, rushed to their aid – but not before leaving a pot of water on the gas stove in order to make a nice cup of hot cocoa for them after the tent had been rendered water-proof and I had provided them with some warm, dry bedding.

Naaaaahhh, not actually…

In fact, the moment I looked out and took in these bizarre goings-on, I exploded in peals of gut wrenching, uncontrollable laughter. I folded over in a fit of mirth of such magnitude it brought me seriously close to doing myself bodily harm. I was incapacitated – the scene was hilarious. When the goings-on in the tent finally stopped – probably out of exhaustion rather than their having achieved anything resembling an acceptable state of dryness – I was fortunately able to re-gather my composure quite quickly. I rolled over and returned to peaceful slumber in preparation for the next day's fishing, the only slight disturbance to my happy snores being the thought of the weather's possible impact on the next day's fishing...

Such self-centred extravagances seem to have a habit of coming home to roost with interest. In the above case mine waited quite a few years until I was once again comfortably tucked in for the night in my newly acquired ute with its bright blue canvas canopy, out on the sand spit beyond the Inskip barge's departure point. I was snoring a satisfied fisherman's snore (deep and vibrant) when down came the rain. It fell in buckets...tubs...and then, it seemed, in swimming pools. And that was *inside* the canopy! God knows what it was doing outside. I didn't stop to look. I was far too pre-occupied with trying to avoid drowning or being washed away. I fumbled frantically for a torch, which fortunately hadn't drowned, and shone it upwards. YE BLOODY GODS AND GODZILLAS! The rain was somehow being *channelled* from outside to *inside* – what the hell sort of design was that? Bloody *heck*!

The back of the ute was awash, and my bedding along with it. *Of course* I hadn't woken up in advance and been able to take preventive measures. Things don't work that way, do they? My healthy snoring had deafened me to the approaching thunder and increasing wind that might have woken me. (External wind, that is, not my own – my own never wakes me up. Others yes, but not me.) I awoke solely in response to extreme wetness – that at least was able to cut unceremoniously through even *my* snoring.

Once the problem was found and its causes determined, I was able to locate a roll of that famous fix-anything silver duct tape and some suitable 'long thin things' to prop up the roof. This had to be done so as to change the slope of the canvas from running into, to running away from, several gaps in the canopy that the manufacturer appeared to have chosen to ignore during its construction. Naturally there would have been no connection between this unfortunate oversight and the urgency I had expressed when ordering it in preparation for my first fishing trip:

"It will be ready *when*? C'MON MAN, you've gotta be *kidding!* I could be *dead* by then! I need it for a fishing trip. Can't you make it sooner? You can? Thanks."

Now I was paying for the twenty-four hours sooner that they had so accommodatingly managed.

By the time the rain stopped I had stemmed the inward flow, and even thought to close up the zip-up windows as well. I didn't sleep any more that night, and discovered next morning that seventy-five millimetres of rain had been measured in the area. Impressive, but a lot less than I estimated for the inside of the back of my ute. Needless to say, I did extensive work of a more permanent nature to the canopy before trusting it to the elements on any subsequent trip. And I was, at least for a short while thereafter, just a smidgen more aware of the risks involved when laughing at others in any predicament in which I might subsequently find myself.

Left: *The offending canvas canopy sharing the limelight with a 15 lb queenfish in better weather (and fishing) conditions.*

Chapter 11

The Beach Corner at Inskip and South West Rocks: Australia Delivers! Big Trevally, Queenfish, Spanish Mackerel, Kingfish... and Strange Fishing Gear

Once I was able to explore the area properly, I found that the place that intrigued and called me most was the point at the sea-end of this sandy stretch. At this corner, out-flowing tidal waters met the ocean in a maelstrom of churning and confused waves, sometimes huge, running for kilometres out to sea. On a rising tide, inflowing oceanic water from the direction of Rainbow Beach flowed with such speed and force that it pushed a long wide column deep into the main flow in or out between Fraser Island and the mainland. This caused a massive mixture of currents and counter currents, all fighting for dominance in an eruption of swirls and waves in all directions.

I had rarely if ever come across an area of sea so active and variable: in the short term from tide to tide, weather pattern to weather pattern, and in the long term by virtue of shifting sand creating large spits and extensive shallows, or deep roaring channels close to the edge. I don't think I had *ever* encountered another system that sang so loudly of the likelihood of big fish.

On my first visit early one morning I just stood and soaked it in, almost in disbelief that a system offering such amazing possibilities could be so easily accessed and fished from the land.

Left: *7 lb tailor caught at night from the beach near the corner. Note the old South African miner's headlamp, still going strong after 25 years of use – and exposure to sea water.*

My curiosity and desire to fish the area was piqued to breaking point and from that moment on I would have given almost anything to live in the beautiful holiday town of Rainbow Beach. Unfortunately commitments such as work (bait and tackle do not grow on trees) allowed me only a few visits to the spot over the next three or four years.

Such was the relative rarity of these visits that I would arrive and stand on the beach, either in the late afternoon or early morning, and stare out over the sand and sea in a state of almost euphoric disbelief and gratitude that I was really here again, free to do as I pleased for the next two or three days.

And such was the intensity of my enthusiasm and curiosity on the earlier visits that I would fish through the night into the early (and sometimes not so early) hours of the morning, usually with two lines out with a live dart (*Trachynotus* sp) on each, to see who was doing the piscatorial night shift. I hooked some big bodies on some of those nights: 'unturnables', even using nearly 350 m of 50 lb line on large Daiwa reels, on which I would have to harden the drag to the max before the line ran out, to ensure it didn't break at the knot on the spool.

I was that keen that I fished even the wintery nights, initially hoping for jewfish. But jewfish never happened. I had heard reports of these fish very occasionally being caught there but they didn't put in an appearance for me – though not for lack of trying on my part. It was so cold on those nights by one or two in the morning when the westerly was blowing that I made myself a huge sheepskin balaclava and hand muffs, in true Robinson Crusoe tradition you could say.

For some strange reason I almost never had any sort of human company in the very early hours of the morning, but there was one exception...

On this cold night the balaclava had been called on to perform its cranial warming duties early in the piece. By about 1.00 am, a spooky time at best, I was facing the sea in pitch darkness when I heard someone approaching from behind. I swung around just as this fellow switched on his torch.

"SHEEE-YIT!" he squawked as the torch beam lit up my balaclava'd countenance. Not surprisingly, mind you. Having frequently inspected myself in the mirror during its manufacture, I was fully aware that the balaclava would have to provide a lot of warmth to make up for what it lacked in beauty. I don't know whose heart came closer to stopping but it must have been a near thing judging by his comments and my shaking – and his eventual laughter when things had settled down a bit and comments about alien attack had ceased.

I understood his surprise well enough under the circumstances, but the persistent titter of laughter did become a trifle peeving, especially as he seemed to be trying desperately to hold it in. A little compliment on the impressive originality of the design (it was *that* at least) and fortitude of the wearer, would have been much better received.

I was never quite comfortable in it after that event, and was quite relieved when my late night excursions petered out due to lack of worthwhile edible fish action, and its services were no longer needed. Most unfortunately I do not have any photographic records, so a drawing will have to suffice.

Every time I managed to visit the corner I would arrive and find the scenario changed. The area of sand spit would alter dramatically, sometimes to an amazing extent. This meant that on each occasion new fishing conditions would have to be accommodated. I recall a visit during one October when a deep, swirling and choppy area with plenty of foamy water formed within easy casting distance of the beach in the very early hours of the morning. For three consecutive mornings, tailor dependably put in an appearance and dropping a bait into that boiling pot would produce a typical feeding attack within seconds. If the attacker was not hooked, the bait would be gone and there was no sense in waiting for more action. The bait would have to be replenished.

The fish would arrive suddenly, stay for twenty or thirty intense fishing minutes, and be gone just as suddenly. I am not a tailor fisherman as such, but they are mighty fine eating, and it was too exciting and fascinating to miss. This particular phenomenon never re-occurred in exactly the same way, but others took its place. I always *hoped* for consistency in these events, but it didn't work out like that. It was almost like fishing a new venue on each occasion.

Queenfish (*Scomberoides commersonianus*) would sometimes turn up each morning for two or three days in calm water at low tide off the beach side of the corner, or big tailor would present themselves in the surf at the turn of a high tide early in the evening. Or giant trevally would be present in the afternoon for a few days at the drop-off on the inside of the corner as a pushing tide carried bait fish over the edge. Then it would be tailor again, which would show up at the bottom of a low tide at 11.00 pm in dead calm water on the inside of the corner, or silver trevally would be in the same area just after dark. After each such event I would go home with that memory, and would arrive the next time anticipating a repeat performance. But this literally never happened – the beach would have changed and there might be sand where before there was sea. Instead, there was always some new phenomenon to discover.

It was wonderful exciting fishing, perhaps even more especially in the early days when I had absolutely *no* idea what might be lurking there, waiting to take a bait.

Left: *"Sometimes the queenies would turn up."* The author with his younger son Chris and a morning's catch.

As mentioned earlier in the book, I had long dreamed of catching a giant trevally from the rocks or beach but never managed to achieve this in South Africa where their habitat was very limited, and access to this habitat even more limited. I was reaching that stage of unhappy acceptance that the dream (or I) might die of old age first. Then just in the nick of time the gods of the deep, sensing the bad vibes coming in their direction, looked down, saw their tragic omission, and took urgent action. The outcome unfolded on one of my earliest trips to the Inskip corner while I was fishing with a pillie in shallow turbulent water well before sunrise, on a glorious windless and cloudless morning – yep, one of *those* days. I was standing knee deep in the churning water, enjoying the surroundings but not the lack of large pilchard-eating fish.

As I stood almost mesmerised by the morning's beauty, a large mullet leapt from the foaming water not five metres from where I was standing and brought me instantly back to reality. The mullet hadn't done that out of *'joie de vivre'* as I myself might have done at the time. No way! It had become airborne thanks to a powerful instinct to survive. It was being pursued, and judging by its own size its pursuer was none too small itself. I was galvanised into action and reeled in my pillie at top speed, then headed for my fishing bag. I dug around in the morass of bits and pieces, nose twitching – I *must* wash that bag sometime. Finally my hand emerged triumphantly holding an old tin spoon bearing the dents of many near misses on rocky surfaces. By comparison this sandy beach would be a holiday for it.

I tied the spoon on hastily, but not too hastily to wet the line and check the knot's strength with a good hard pull or two. Thus equipped I headed back to the water at top speed, almost plunging headlong into the waves as they tried hard to push my legs in the opposite direction. Balancing myself against the waist-deep waves, I swung the spoon back and flung it with full force in a wide low arc, careful to avoid whipping it smack into the sea behind me. Such an eventuality would almost definitely have produced a violent over-wind (bird's nest) which would have been disastrous under these time-critical circumstances. Groups of big fish tend to move on and not stick around, though this and future interludes with the species in question proved them to be quite exceptional in this respect.

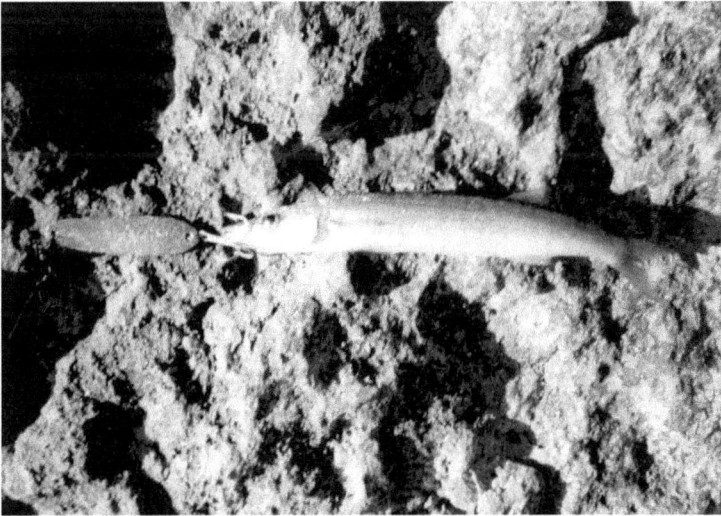

Above: *An example of a battered tin spoon taken by an enthusiastic tin-eater of less than three times the spoon's own length*

After a clean flight of over a hundred metres, the spoon hit the water with a barely visible splash and the retrieve began. I had straightened the soft tin spoon so there was little resistance and I retrieved it rapidly through the white, foamy and relatively shallow water. What on earth could be operating in *that* water which was large enough to be chasing such big mullet? Big fish often enough chase

251

prey into shallow water, but so rough and foamy? The old adrenalin was doing its thing of course. The retrieve ended without excitement, and the sun was about to poke its nose above the horizon.

Out went the spoon again in that familiar beautiful huge arc as it had done so many hundreds of times for me in the past, with not even a slight wobble to disrupt its passage. Again it fell and hit the water. Again I took up the slack and began the paced retrieve. On this second throw, after just two or three turns of the spool, the spoon was attacked in what felt like a hook-up on solid rock. I instinctively hit and hit again, hard. There was no reaction, just dead weight, literally like hooking a rock or log. Then it began to move away, no jerk, no tugging, no head-shaking, just a slow but increasing movement away from me. What the hell could this be? There were a few possibilities vaguely ticking over in my mind, but still being fairly new to the spot I had no real idea as to the extent of its potential in variety of species.

What I *did* know for certain is that it wasn't a log. Its speed increased progressively as advantage was taken of the incoming tide's powerful flow away from me, which the fish reached as it moved beyond the shallows. Whatever the fish was, it had an enormous advantage in this – really bad for me.

By virtue of 'Murphy's law', at the time I happened to be using a much smaller and lighter reel than the Shimano SpeedMaster I normally used. It was a good light spinning reel but was really too small for its present application, holding rather too little 30 lb line for the task at hand. Furthermore on a few occasions the line had found its way between the spool and the reel housing, causing some damage to the line which was now giving me nightmares, and which caused me to abandon the reel altogether shortly thereafter. Right now I was having one of those horrible regrets at not having grabbed the Speedmaster when I knew that the fish I was dealing with were substantial. Fortunately on this occasion my error was not disastrous.

Very rapidly I realized that old familiar heart-palpitating need for maximum pressure as the fish moved ever further away in the swirling current – very stressful, as I *really* wanted to know what it was. Fortunately for me, it is amazing just how strong lighter line can be relative to heavy line which will sometimes break at the knot under unexpectedly low strain considering its claimed strength. Quite inexplicable, though pulling knots tight without wetting them can cause this to happen. Anyway, the reel, thinner line and I all hung in there on this occasion.

There was still no jerking, just a steady heavy pull. The line was still on its way out, though it slowed a bit from time to time, which was heartening. Nevertheless, there was worrisomely little line left and I was having a bad nervous sweat. But Lady Luck eventually put in an appearance and the outward trend ground to a halt before disaster could strike – a small miracle under the circumstances. The very occasional head shake or bump at the other end told me the fish was trying different tactics. I began *very* carefully to retrieve line by lifting the rod slowly and winding as the rod was lowered again, incredibly carefully so as not to jerk or scare the fish into another run which could have ended it all. I heaved a sigh of relief with every metre so regained. Every bit was just a little more insurance against another run being able to do 'terminal damage'.

However as was to be expected, after a while when the fish sensed the water becoming shallower, runs against the drag began again. There were quite a few of them: powerful, determined and quite sustained, meaning that quite a lot of hard-earned line was lost each time, but never again to the extent that I felt the threat of being stripped. As always, as the fish got closer and the situation grew progressively safer, I reduced the drag to minimize the chance of the line breaking. That high degree of vigilance and constant attention to what was happening every moment, and preparedness to instantly let the fish run if necessary, never declined. I was on intense high alert, a state which only copious amounts of adrenalin and past losses can produce.

As more and more line was won back and the fish drew closer, its fight, though becoming progressively less powerful, became more dynamic, with turns and bumps and arcing from left to right. I had moved towards the left, up the beach to where a fairly large swell was peaking and breaking in a dump right at the sea's edge. Although the fish was quite close, this wave action and sudden drop-off made spotting it difficult, all the more so as it fought deep, so I still had no idea what it was. I made several attempts to use a breaking swell to lift it in over the drop-off into shallower white water from which beaching it would be relatively easier, but it made this extremely difficult by positioning its body side-on to maximize resistance.

The final moments were taken up with persuading the fish to come in over this sandy drop-off, and once over, holding it as hard as I dared against the backwash and against its relentless swimming efforts. This was achieved on a couple of occasions only to have the backwash suck it alarmingly back down – just as I thought the war was over. On about the third attempt to lift it over I managed to hold it there and as the broken wave subsided, I recognised it as a giant trevally – the fish I had been dreaming of for so many years. A few more moments using low broken waves to move it in my direction, and the fish was safely beached.

I was immediately hit with an intense burst of incredulity, relief and gratitude – collectively euphoric. I recall no more intense moment in my fishing career, before or since.

I had my two young sons with me at the time. They were in camp, having decided that the hour of day was better suited to bed than beach. I carried the fish back to camp. *That* woke them up! After placing the fish in the shade I headed straight back to the beach and my rod. The fight would have lasted well over half an hour, the sun was up and I figured a repeat was pretty unlikely – but hope springs eternal…

As I was not using a steel trace, in case of wear and tear on the last few inches of line I retied the knot. Out went the spoon again. Amazingly, two or three throws later and WHACK! I was in again.

This fight was more active but with a shorter initial run – though there most certainly was one. However there was no danger of being stripped on this occasion, and after a somewhat shorter total time, which included more short runs and head jerking than the first fish, it was pulled up over the drop-off into shallower water using a swell. Seconds thereafter the spoon fell from its mouth. It was still very much alive and flapping in water still easily deep enough for an escape bid. I dropped the rod and rushed to secure it, placing my left hand hard on its body and grabbing its caudal peduncle (the thin section in front of the tail) with my right hand, holding it as firmly as I could while the spiky scutes along its sides made their presence felt in no uncertain terms.

Left: *The first GTs of 33 lb and 27 lb, on spoon at the Inskip beach corner.*

As soon as the water permitted I dragged it to the safety of higher ground. A second big trevally in one morning; I could scarcely believe it. WHEW, WHAT A DAY! A DREAM COME TRUE. YOU *BEAUDY*! They weighed in at 33 and 27 lb respectively.

Above: *The corner, with sea conditions almost identical to those when the first trevally were caught. Fraser Island is in the background.*

One of the first things I exploited when fishing this spot was the tidal flow, both in and out, to carry live-baits to deep water. This phenomenon, whereby currents or other elements can be used to carry bait from shallow to deep water, is relatively rare if one considers all fishing venues. The value of such an opportunity, especially if it is reliable, is enormous to any angler who chooses this way of fishing.

Examples include tidal flows such as the beach end of Inskip, river mouths, off-shore winds from suitable spots, and more rarely, obliging currents which flow away from suitable rocky sites. The great beauty with Inskip beach is the easy access to this phenomenon, which can be exploited with both incoming and outgoing tides, though outgoing is somewhat better.

Two serious negatives do impact here though. Firstly if there is weed around, this naturally causes problems, and secondly only one fisherman can comfortably exploit the situation at any one time as the current will quickly tangle more than one line.

One can often stand directly in the extremely strong current, which means that a minimal cast will suffice, though it is usually beneficial to throw the bait some distance. It is also essential to hook the live-bait securely through its upper jaw, rather than elsewhere. This allows it to swim upright even in a very strong flow. In a strong flow, a hook in the back will cause spinning which will twist the line and kill the bait. I stood on many occasions for hours with live-baits out, retrieving them still healthy and kicking when they were eventually checked, enabling me to release them alive if they were not found by a big predator.

Generally the best time/tidal situation for this is a high tide very early in the morning, such that the water is already just running out as it gets light. This enables the phenomenon to be exploited for the longest possible time, in optimum fishing time – early morning. Significantly, in this particular water big fish can still be encountered quite late into the morning, which makes it even more unusual, as game fish often feed most actively from first light to a little after sunrise and then tail off – at least in land-based fishing. I would often stand at this particular venue for three or even four hours on a summer morning. Such long fishing periods might deliver anywhere from zero to three or four pick-ups max.

Right: *Another of the corner's beautiful GTs, this one weighing in at 31 lb.*

In the late afternoon things can pick up again. I have hooked a number of good queenfish at that time, though again often with very long waits in between pick-ups. Probably the vast majority of fishermen would not bother to invest so much effort and time for such infrequent action. Such is the lot of the land-based fisherman in search of big fish.

Of course, although there are no rocks to devour one's tackle here, many of the other forces causing fish to be lost still remain in play. I recall with unpleasant clarity how one beautiful late afternoon I had managed to put all of the pieces of the angling jigsaw puzzle together: a good live-bait, positioned well out on the less-easy-to-work-with incoming tide, in perfect conditions. Here at least, the queenies definitely seemed to favour moderately calm though slightly choppy water (the chop being caused by light counter currents) over which a late afternoon sun was shining. I was using a new batch of line which had already caused a raised eyebrow due to knots breaking when tested after tying – despite being wetted when tying them.

I waited a while, expectantly (as always) but with a piqued sense of anticipation as a result of the superb conditions. After a while there was that familiar 'tug, tug' of a disturbed live-bait, and 'off she went'. I conducted the normal nerve-wracking wait to allow for swallowing, then struck three or four times. Immediately the startled fish leapt from the water, fell back and took off in the opposite direction. It was a beauty, and with the water flow favouring it a little, I tightened up. This again caused a jump or two from the fish – an exciting aspect of queenies' display. I hadn't turned it yet, when all of a sudden for absolutely no apparent reason, the line went slack. My heart did the dreaded 'lost-fish-palpitation' as I rapidly retrieved line to see if by some miracle the fish had turned and come towards me. But no, a moment later it leapt again, still moving in the opposite direction and I knew it was all over.

My unhappy memory is of that beautiful fish leaping off into the gorgeous afternoon sunshine, doubtless with a broad grin on its face. The line had broken without apparent rhyme or reason and I ripped it unceremoniously off the reel and replaced it with something more trustworthy. Too late for that fish though.

On a subsequent trip things panned out more favourably. It was late afternoon, with the tide running out from a high which had just turned. The sand spit had created an unusually deep channel running very close to the edge, an occurrence which would only last until the dropping water emptied it. I had a seventeen or eighteen centimetre dart out live. It had settled well, out in deeper 'humpy' water, quite turbulent though not foamy – more active than I would usually have associated with queenfish.

Fortunately, despite the water's motion, the bait stayed in its excellent position for long enough for a fish to find it – a queenfish as it happened. They are excellent fish from a fighting perspective (and not bad tucker either) and this fellow was no exception. Not long and it made things clear it was a good fish, with a strong run terminating in several high leaps. Great to watch even if somewhat nerve-wracking, though the chances of a single hook being thrown are far lower than when using a lure. Landing presented no exceptional circumstances or sweating and the fish weighed in at seventeen and a half pounds. Unfortunately fish of this size tend only to happen infrequently, with many smaller ones in between. Never mind, it's all good practice.

Right: *17.5 lb queenfish on live dart.*

It is perhaps fitting to end the book's fishing stories with one of the finest episodes of my entire fishing career, before relaxing my typing fingers (one on each hand) for the last time. Well, unless another tale comes to mind that simply can't be left out.

The event took place over two days, in February 2001. On the first day I landed a giant trevally of 28 lb on a live dart in the standard fashion; that is, by sending the bait out on an outgoing tide early in the morning. The following morning I had just arrived on the beach side of the corner and was fishing knee deep in small waves and quite clear water – not much foam, and the water itself was warm and crystal clear. All of a sudden I saw several large mullet streak by at top speed seeking refuge in shallow water. They were clearly not casually looking for a quiet place to eat breakfast.

Behind them, also at top speed, followed a large trevally. It *was* looking for breakfast. It passed within two or three metres of my legs, either unaware of or totally ignoring my presence. I felt the old adrenalin rush as the trevally swerved, having missed the mullet, and made for the sanctuary of deeper water. With a sense of anticipation and at a speed at least equalling that of the trevally, I wound my live-bait back from where the strong current had deposited it, a long way out. As usual this was still alive and active, and I flicked it into the water about ten metres in front of me. I waited barely seconds before a trevally picked up the bait and roared off, no questions asked.

I hit solidly and the game was on. The fish streaked off and made for the open sea, the reel losing nylon at a hair-raising rate. I was using a Shimano SpeedMaster IV, which most fortunately held a generous amount of 35 lb line. But that was one of the longest non-stop runs (other than by big sharks) that I had ever experienced. It is too easy to sound clichéd when saying that I damned nearly ran out of line, but I damn well nearly did. This has not exactly been a rarity over the years.

By the time the fish had exploited the movement of the out-flowing water, then turned right and run down the beach towards the town of Rainbow Beach, I had precious little bargaining power left. The spool was literally almost empty and I had substantially reduced the drag to accommodate the remaining line's shrunken diameter, which proportionately increases the amount of pull needed to release line, so this reduction in drag was essential to avoid a bust up. Enough drag to hold the fish as hard as safely possible but not enough to break it – a constant balancing act. It was only because the fish chose to move parallel to the coast and not straight out to sea that I was able to follow it along the beach and avoid running out of line – very fortunate indeed.

On such occasions after a powerful first run, the turning of the fish and the spool's first few turns of line recovery are always accompanied by indescribable relief. In land-based fishing, if the line runs out it simply snaps unless one is almost miraculously fortunate in still being able to turn the fish before this happens – very rare. In this case, as usual I breathed a sigh of relief for every retrieving turn of the spool until I knew that I had regained enough line to weather another good run if necessary. At this point, provided I kept up the pressure and no other untoward events intervened, I was winning.

From memory, the fight must have lasted somewhere between thirty and forty minutes (it certainly felt that long) before the fish was subdued sufficiently to persuade it to enter the calm, clear, shallow sandy stretch of water that lay between it and myself – a distance of about 50 metres. I never gaffed in these circumstances (on my own and landing a fish on a beach), so the fish always had to be totally subdued and brought into shallow water before it was safe to hold the rod in one hand (in case of a last dash by the fish) and attempt to find secure purchase on the fish's body with the other. To attempt this in deeper water with one hand would be very risky – far better to exercise patience and bring the fish into water in which it could no longer swim upright, though this still did not mean there was absolutely no chance it would dash along on its side in a last bid to get away.

When the fish was finally landed and carried up the beach, its eye-catching potential immediately attracted the attention of an elderly couple driving by on an otherwise deserted stretch of coastline. After initial gasps, exclamations and questions, they kindly offered to photograph the fish on the spot using the camera which I happened to have with me. This was most fortuitous as the picture captured the prevailing remarkably calm sea conditions for reference. The trevally weighed 42 lb.

Right: *The 42 lb giant trevally. Note calm conditions and live-bait containers.*

By this time the tide was well and truly out and there was no possibility of launching another bait as the flow had stopped. So I returned to camp, cleaned the fish and delivered it to the ever-obliging Dean's Ice in the town of Rainbow Beach, to join the previous day's capture in their cold storage facility. I then returned to camp and the shade of the casuarinas to enjoy a snooze out of the beating sun before rising and setting off for the afternoon shift.

When I did eventually break away from dreamland and dance down to the beach it was around two in the afternoon. Dance? By that time of day the sand was 'king' hot and I was barefooted. Hence the dance. (If you are a purist and don't like the term 'dance' then please feel free to replace it with hopped or whatever.) What I *didn't* do was *stroll*. SHEE-IT, NO! I moved as fast as my legs would carry me, while doing everything in my power to minimize contact between soles of feet and sizzling sand. Only the first one or two steps would have revealed any effort on my part to avoid looking utterly stupid. Thereafter it was a shameless hop, skip and jump, regardless!

I'm sure there was hissing and steam as I hopped into the sole-saving sea water to cool down. SHIT-A-HOT-BRICK, it was a relief. Queensland can get *pretty* warm in February.

By the time I reached the corner, the tide was running in at full tilt. It had, on this trip, created yet another hitherto unseen formation in the sand. Incoming water was running northwards along the beach until it rushed over a sandy drop-off into the deep turbulent blue water of the inlet, producing yet another extraordinarily fishy looking patch of ocean. Beyond this drop-off, swells and waves were rising and falling in all directions, swells lifting into breaking crests then falling into deep troughs. Despite the less-than-optimum hour of day for spinning (throwing a spoon), the water looked so good that I couldn't resist tying on a spoon and having a few throws.

I wish I could have video'd the outcome. On about the third throw a massive trevally launched itself at my spoon (which was being retrieved just below the surface), with such force that it exploded from the water in a leap of several feet. This took place within metres of the steep drop-off and was one of those mind-blowing piscatorial incidents that leave one well and truly gob-smacked. Shaking my head partly in disbelief and partly to reseat my eyeballs in their sockets, I cast again, thinking that the same or another fish would *have* to strike if that was the mood they were in.

Against my expectations, nothing happened, and after five or six more actionless throws I packed it in and grabbed my little live-bait rod in the hope of catching some dart. That at least presented no problem, and before long out went the first live dart with its short-shank hook braced for business.

The hook didn't have long to wait. I doubt whether it was more than two minutes before the live-bait was hit by something that felt more like an underwater locomotive than a fish. Off it went with pace and power I reckon I could have skied behind. Once again it had a potent tidal flow in its favour and yet again here I was watching the line diameter on my spool reducing at an alarming rate. As was now the norm, I was using the Shimano SpeedMaster and although the fish certainly stripped plenty of line before turning, there was no real perspiration-producing loss of line during the scrap. As is usual for this powerful species though, it was tenacious, dogged and unrelenting. They are simply magnificent. This fellow weighed 34 lb.

Out went another live-bait and again within just a few minutes, a trevally and I were battling it out. This was a smaller specimen of about 18 lb, which after photographing it against my nylon live-bait bin, I released alive.

I had enough fish by then and although I am sure there would have been more, I decided to hit the road, my trip being at an end that day. It was an incredible period of fishing. These fish really do seem to congregate in a suitable area and hang out there for a while, presumably for as long as the food fish are available. The catch for the two days was four fish: 18, 28, 34 and 42 lb. Could've been worse!

Above: *Giant trevally, estimated at 18 lb, posing briefly next to a live-bait container.*

* * *

Stop press – late addition!

Well, it's happened. Another two stories that *cannot* be left out have happened, and I've had to recall both of my typing fingers from their hard-earned retirement.

The first good fish was landed just as I was literally within days of sending this complete (or so I thought) manuscript for perusal by the publishing fraternity. It wouldn't have happened if my dear wife hadn't encouraged me to visit the corner of Inskip after several years of absence. (True story! Eat your hearts out guys.) Who was I to argue? On Friday, 9 February 2007 at about 2.00 pm, I left for the fishing grounds.

It just so happened that there was, prior to this catch, another long-standing omission on the part of the gods of fishing in filling my angling desires. However, at the time of my departure, this missing link in my fishing records was far from my thoughts. After my earlier magical catches of big trevally I didn't dare approach the gods again. I could just hear them saying, "Our hearts pump crystallised camel-snot for you, Boy!" So I left things to chance – no sense in being greedy.

I arrived at about 4.00 pm in a different vehicle from the trusty old Navara and immediately got bogged twenty metres up the access road because I had stupidly said to myself, "I'll easily get up here without dropping the tyre pressure. She'll be right." Of course prime fishing time was fast approaching and I immediately resorted to bad language to boost my digging efforts. Happily, a gent in a passing vehicle saw my plight and pulled me out backwards, quickly getting me on my way. I was almost (but not quite) in too much of a hurry to feel embarrassed.

Upon arrival on the beach I geared up to catch dart for live-bait in the hope of attracting the attention of a queenfish. The water was as good as I'd ever seen it, dropping off deep right at the edge of the sand, all the way round the corner. You beauty! What I didn't know until my dart bait hit the water is that the dreaded brown algae referred to in the area as 'weed' was present. *Very bad* news. The first headache it produced was to interfere with catching dart which is normally easy in the white water at the sea's edge. Most fortunately as it turned out, the weed wasn't especially bad at that point in time and I was able not only to catch a dart but to get it to stay out without drifting once it was rigged as a live-bait. With the rod secured in a holder in the sand, drag set low and ratchet engaged, I went about catching another dart or two which would be kept alive in a bucket.

Some moments later the rod dipped enthusiastically in the holder, the ratchet chirped – then nothing. Damn! I reeled in to find the hook bitten off. "Blooming shark," was my instant response. They are common thieves of live-bait there and a considerable nuisance when dart are being difficult to catch. I rigged up another bait and held the rod this time. After just a few minutes it went the same way. I didn't want sharks but I didn't feel like letting them get away with my hard-earned live-baits, so I decided, all things considered, that I might as well put a steel trace on and get some exercise.

I didn't even bother to hold the rod, but put it in the holder again and continued my quest for dart. I had pretty much forgotten about it when the rod started doing its bend-over dance to the music of a very excited ratchet. By force of habit I leapt over and grabbed it, dropping and abandoning my dart-catching outfit in the rush. Whatever had made the enquiry remained interested and off it went in that nerve-wracking way that they do. I disengaged the ratchet, freed the spool and let the fish run. It ran for a few seconds, stopped briefly then took off again. Time to teach it not to steal live-bait. I quickly tightened the drag while the spool was still spinning freely, snapped the lever over to engage the spool, waited for the rod to pull down and hit several times to show it who was boss. It took off in the opposite direction, evidently with the intent of showing me the same thing. The run was steady and long but not exceptionally fast. The fish stopped a couple of times but could not be turned, and headed out again on each occasion after a moment's delay.

Eventually after taking close to two thirds of the reel's line it stopped, and I was able to commence retrieval by walking backwards up the sand – a very useful option, but one almost never available when playing a fish from the rocks. The tactic's main advantage lies in enabling line to be retrieved smoothly with no repeated lifting of the rod against the fish followed by downward movement while reeling in line. This jerky action can easily scare the fish into extending its run. Up until then there had been little active movement or jerking by the fish; more of a strong steady pull. This continued with little change though there were occasional determined turns and runs as it approached the beach, until in the approaching darkness it could be lifted up over the prevailing steep sandy drop-off.

The moment I recognised it I hit a new high in amazement and delight – a Spanish mackerel (*Scomberomorus commersoni*). What an absolute beauty! I had never landed a big one from the land and this was a wonderful prize. I knew mackerel of all kinds patrolled the passage but I had never made contact. The nature of its fight had certainly not prompted me to think in that direction.

Some nearby observers kindly offered to take a photograph on the spot; did I have a camera? I sure did, and I would fetch a scale as well.

I immediately discovered I didn't have a scale with me. While I smoothed back my hair and checked my teeth for the photo, a young lass in the group got the camera ready. I struck a suitable pose and she hit the button. There should have been a flash as by then it was almost dark. Instead the camera made a slight buzzing sound and a click. No amount of pushing and pulling could get it to produce the required indications that a photograph had been successfully taken. Bugger! This and the fact that I didn't have a scale with me meant the fish had to go home intact. I thanked the would-be photographer for her efforts and headed towards Rainbow Beach to seek out the only person I knew there: Syd Smith, whom I had met when he operated the 'Munch Mobile' and who had kindly frozen big fish for me in years gone by.

After being told by a local café owner that he had moved house, I knocked at the wrong door before finding the right house. There was nobody there, but I was then told by some very fortuitous chance arrivals at the house (while I was bruising my fist on its solid front door) that he was down at the club. Where's that? They offered to show me the way there by getting me to follow them in their car. I eventually found Syd about to have an evening meal with a female friend. That was only after first being told I couldn't go into the club barefoot, and having to adjust my attire to meet protocol. I obviously wanted very badly to keep the fish in photogenic condition.

Typically friendly and helpful, Syd temporarily abandoned his friend and pending meal, and escorted me back to his house to put the fish into the deepfreeze. "Anytime," he said. "No problem." How good was that? So happily, thanks to Syd, I have a photograph. The fish weighed thirty-one pounds.

The second afternoon produced no edibles and conditions with the weed were bad. All three mornings were almost unfishable, though there were still fish around. On the third afternoon the dart were back and so were the mackerel. The initial choice was to target queenfish again, and hence no steel trace was used as they tend to be put off by it. I was fishing on the ocean side of the corner where the weed situation was slightly better than on the bank facing Fraser Island. Late in the afternoon after having no action there, I decided to test a live-dart in the part of the system where I had caught the mackerel, about one hundred metres away. Action would have to happen very quickly or the weed would foul the line.

Within seconds of the bait hitting the water it was attacked and cut off. Mackerel! I saw one leaping high into the air a hundred metres or so away and leapt in the opposite direction myself to grab my second rod, already made up with a steel trace

Left: *31 lb Spanish Mackerel, with Shimano SpeedMaster IV on home-built rod.*

Right: *The business end of the mackerel.*

Within a minute or so of hitting the water the next bait-fish was picked up and my entire trace – sinker, steel wire, hooks and all – was bitten off. Third live-bait out, and within the same sort of time frame this was chopped off just behind the hook. What to do now? I had no more live-bait. Instead of trying to catch more I decided to try a pillie on gang hooks. After a short wait this was hit and I missed the strike. Then it was all over – not another touch. The action can be hot when it's happening but big fish don't come easily for the shore-based angler.

PS: If the folks who offered and then attempted to photograph the mackerel ever happen to read this, the reason that the camera was not performing properly was simple. It had no film in it. That's why I haven't advanced from fishing to photography.

The second late story is about one that got away. That is, one that got away after being dead for two hours. That's what makes it unusual and worth including at this advanced stage.

It happened after a relocation to live in the village of South West Rocks in New South Wales, a move made at least partly for its excellent fishing. South West Rocks offered what new areas always offer: the fascination of discovering what fish live there, using a fishing rod to find out. I arrived in winter, the quietest fishing time of the year. Nevertheless, within just a few weeks spinning from the rocks had delivered numerous small trevally, some good sized tailor, a five pound mac tuna, a ten pound kingfish (and numerous released undersized kingies), and the beaches had delivered around half a dozen Australian salmon of five to six pound, an 11 lb jewfish, and a number of released undersized jewfish.

A few months after I had moved there, I discovered an interesting and promising fishing spot on one of its main beaches, very close to the mouth of the magnificent Macleay River. This made a pleasant change from clambering over large rocks in the dark to get to or return from any one of several extremely promising looking areas where I had been trying for some time to connect with a big kingfish (*Seriola lalandi*), using a spoon (lure), at dawn or dusk.

The beach spot was a long but easy walk, and there were several superb gutters in the surf which always seemed to be there. I had had consistently good catches of smaller edibles in the area up to about 10 lbs, but was looking for specimens of over 20 lbs. (For conversational and photographic reasons, if you get my drift: "Got a real beauty the other day, have a look at this...")

Anyway, one afternoon after a northerly wind had been howling for a day or two and was still doing so, and the sea was wild, the decision was made to go out and try to introduce myself to a big jewfish. They favour a very active and preferably discoloured sea, so despite the difficult fishing conditions, I gritted my teeth and headed seawards.

Although the plan was to fish at night – all night if it seemed worthwhile – I went out at about 4.00 pm with the intention of catching some fresh baitfish before dark, rather than expecting big jewfish to lower themselves to eating pilchards. I baited up with a whole pillie in the hope of attracting a tailor or Australian salmon, both of which when filleted extremely fresh are *very* palatable to jewfish. After a few casts, during which I watched the sinker extremely carefully until it hit the water for fear it might be blown back at me by the howling wind and knock me out, I became reconciled to using pilchards for the jewfish after all. Barely a touch on the baits, and certainly nothing significant. Then suddenly and unexpectedly (which is *actually* when we fishermen *should* expect such things), a denizen picked up the pillie. With the usual instant adrenaline rush, I waited for the fish to pull the rod down sufficiently to get good leverage for striking and to give it time to swallow...*or* spit the bait out, which so often happens instead. No spitting out this time, so I introduced myself to it with three or four hefty strikes.

This is always a critical moment. Would the hooks set? They did. The strikes hit solid resistance (beauty!) and the fish went wild, screeching off, taking line, stopping, jerking, then running again. Suddenly to my horror, the line went slack. *Oh no!* Hooks pulled out. *THAT* again! To my enormous relief (which happens far less often...), as I wound in the slack line I found that the fish had in fact swum in towards me, right into the foaming and boiling surf. Realizing its navigational error, hardly surprising in the circumstances unless it had radar, it turned around, took up the remaining slack line and roared off out to sea at an alarming rate. It raced on non-stop for a worrisome distance and amount of fishing line.

To turn the fish, I kept the rod steady and the drag at a safe tension, making it work as hard as possible without risking breaking the line, simultaneously avoiding any jerking movements which would spur it on. (As mentioned earlier in the book, the latter is a useful and effective technique for helping to reduce the risk of having a reel stripped completely by a big fish.) Fortunately there were no rocks or other snags, so those potential threats were absent – a wonderful situation.

The fish finally slowed to a stop, and as always when fishing on the beach I held steady until I could start to walk backwards to retrieve line, still avoiding any jerking on the line. When I had moved back a sufficient distance, I began to move forwards again, carefully winding in to recover line. This first recovery of line after a long run is always a great relief and signals a turn of the tables in the fight. Thereafter the fish moved in a large arc but rarely took line again, until it discovered the drop-off and shallow water which immediately scared it into renewed activity. By this time the drag had been reduced substantially – no need to keep maximum pressure any longer – and the fight remained give-and-take until the fish could be beached.

For all of this time, some fifteen or twenty minutes, I had absolutely no idea what it could be. Too active for a shark considering its wide arcs and relentless powerful pull (and a nylon trace which a shark would have severed), and far too fast and vigorous for a jewfish, even a big one. Also different from the very powerful and dogged, but somewhat slower fight of a large shovelnose. The first clue was the pointed fins of a pelagic species finally appearing above the white water in the shallows. *BRILLIANT!* Not a shark. Over and over the fish was held as it fought to use the backwash to its advantage. Slowly the final few metres of line were recovered until a large kingfish lay stranded and clearly visible. A *kingfish!* In that wild, shallow water! It was unbelievable, but that is one of the things that make fishing so fascinating – the unexpected.

I then did something which is very unusual for me. After delivering a lethal incision to the fish, I took out a camera and photographed it and the remarkable surf conditions in which it had been hooked.

Then I went back to fishing in the still howling wind. Nothing happened fish-wise, but weather-wise an electric storm was fast approaching – no wonder the fishing was dead. At about 8.00 pm I reluctantly decided to pack it in and go home. It was almost dark by this time and a headlamp was needed. Tackle packed up, I lifted the kingfish, which I estimated to be at least 25 lbs in weight, and took it to the water to gut it. And that was where *DISASTER* struck. Twice the rush of the waves and wash twisted the heavy fish out of my grip. The first time it happened I retrieved it from the wash, and continued with gutting. You would have thought I would have seen the risk. The second time it was wrenched free by the rush of a larger passing wave, close to the drop-off into deeper water. With the swim bladder removed it sank like a stone and disappeared instantly into the turmoil and turbulence, and darkness. Frantically I thrashed around in the water, searching in vain with the headlamp's beam, hoping the fish would be washed ashore. That didn't happen. The fish was nowhere to be found, carried rapidly back out over the drop-off by the powerful wash. *GONE!* Unbelievable. Half of my brain was working at preventing a heart attack and the other was unhappily observing a new depth of disbelief.

Above: *The sea, photographed minutes after the kingfish was landed. Who would expect a kingie in* that *water? About two hours later, in the dark, and with the tide much higher, the fish was reclaimed by the sea.*

I walked up and down the beach at the surf's edge, searching and hoping, but I knew with heavy heart that with the prevailing strong offshore rip, my fish was already on its way to New Zealand, this time by virtue of Mother Nature's navigational control rather than its own. I am sure it fattened many a marine animal's belly that night, but to date I've had no letters of thanks.

It is of little consolation to me that this event may constitute some sort of record, as in: "Largest fish ever lost in Australia after being dead for two hours." But how fortuitous that it had been captured on film. Imagine presenting such an unlikely fisherman's story with no hard evidence! What was also fortunate is that it was purposely photographed next to one of my fishing rods, to show its size. This enabled the length to be measured surprisingly accurately, using marks on the rod. The total length was 110 cm, with a fork length of very close to 105 cm. Using the DPI's very useful length-to-weight conversion chart, a kingfish with a fork length of 105 cm will on average weigh 14.8 kg or 32.5 lb. My estimate had been at least 25 lbs, so along with the DPI figure, and the fact that the fish was relatively slender – probably recently spawned – my best estimate would be between 27 and 30 lbs.

There is an ironic twist to this tale. Two nights later I was fishing the same spot in the same conditions…in the vain hope of a repeat of the amazing earlier catch. But all I was catching was large fork-tailed catfish. I returned these alive, and here was the irony. Despite being strongly alive, they kept washing *back* up onto the beach from which I had to rescue them and release them again into deeper water, until apparently by chance they headed off in the right direction.

Above: *The kingfish, photographed next to a fishing rod with a Shimano SpeedMaster reel. Note the manufacturer's logo on the rod (white mark) which corresponds roughly with the tip of the fish's tail. The distance from the beginning of the black part of the rod on the left of the reel to the white logo mark is 110 cm.*

That couldn't have happened with my beautiful kingfish of course, oh no. Neptune himself would have made sure it didn't!

Part Three: On Fishing From The Rocks

Chapter 12

Some Suggestions For Staying Alive on the Rocks While Fishing

Above: *A magnificent looking spot for throwing a spoon – but does it meet the safety criteria? If it can't be fished safely, or if a fish can't be landed safely from it, the spot is only good for looking at or photographing. (Photo courtesy of Mike Thom.)*

This was never intended to be a 'How To' book, but one way or another it ended up containing so many examples of 'how *not* to' that to achieve a little balance, I decided to add some positive suggestions.

Rock fishing is regarded as one of the world's most dangerous sports, but the sea is only as dangerous to us as we allow it to be. Safety awareness is of paramount importance. Many difficult places *can* be fished safely if they are approached in the correct way: with a knowledge of the sea, a level head, a strong sense of caution and above all the ability to resist temptation and say, "No, I am not going to fish there today, it's too dangerous."

Here are some thoughts on the matter and actions that can be taken to improve one's chances of catching good fish off the rocks *and* staying alive to fish another day.

Experience and Some Thoughts on So-Called 'Rogue Waves'

The best protection against rock fishing accidents is **knowledge** and a **comprehensive understanding of the sea's behaviour, especially wave action**, gained by **experience**. This gives us a bit of a catch 22 situation – one has to do it to gain experience, but one shouldn't be doing it without experience. The obvious solution is for a beginner *only to undertake rock fishing under the guidance of a responsible, very experienced person.*

I have often watched TV footage of the sea when searches were being conducted for missing fishermen who had been washed off the rocks. I cannot recall a single incident where I haven't thought to myself: why on earth were they fishing from the rocks in those obviously dangerous conditions? I believe that a lack of experience, in particular a lack of understanding of the sea and wave action, is to blame for the majority of accidents.

I am dubious about blaming so-called rogue waves for disasters – almost as though they sneak up unexpectedly with intent, and are unavoidable. Is there really any such thing as a *rogue* wave, except for the rare oceanic phenomena where huge ships get sunk, or tsunamis? From a rock angler's perspective, exceptional waves, changing wave patterns, periodic sets of larger waves and occasional individual bigger-than-average waves (sometimes very much bigger) are the *rule* – we *know* they occur, and they should be anticipated at any time, rather than being described afterwards as something that happened unexpectedly. This is the safest approach. In addition to this, a **greater variability** and **unpredictability** in waves and their size ***can be expected as swell-size and roughness of the sea increase. Swells tend to approach consistently from a particular quarter or angle, for instance a constant swell from the south-west after a south-westerly blow. However, if a strong south-westerly blow is followed by a strong south-easterly blow, cross-swells are likely to develop with considerably increased variability and unpredictability.***

The best way therefore to take the 'rogue' out of any waves is to anticipate trouble – to acknowledge that sudden bigger-than-average waves can happen anytime and the rougher the sea, the greater the likelihood. To guard against this, a *big* margin of safety must be allowed *above* the margin of safety needed for the average size of waves prevailing at any particular time. **Note, *very importantly*, that waves are also significantly more 'aggressive' (for want of a better term) when the tide is coming in (making).**

These are *must knows* for rock fishermen. And that's just the beginning...

General Safety Considerations

The following is a list of points to consider. Note that many of the aspects listed are practical as well as safety related, and may be repeated. Note also that this list is not claimed to be complete, nor do the suggestions by any means guarantee safety – they are included purely for the help they may offer. Naturally many venues can be assessed at a glance to be safe in some respects, but if there is any doubt then a more studious assessment is essential. The checks below may appear complicated but with repetition most become quick and virtually instinctive.

1.   The Venue

▪ **Assessment of the venue** is *critical. Before* going onto any rock fishing spot, consider the following safety aspects. Of course some spots are worse than others – some are very safe, some potentially dangerous; the skill lies in being able to assess this and act accordingly.

Aspects to assess:

▪ **How easy is the area to access?** It may be possible to get down to, but can one get out again – in a hurry if necessary? If one slips, what happens? Does one fall into the sea, or break one's neck on rocks below? Is it really worth the risk – there are, after all, other places.

▪ **Can the spot be easily and safely accessed, and returned from,** at all *tides?* While fishing, especially on a rising tide, this should be constantly monitored if it is potentially an issue. Could breaking waves cause problems? How do tides or slippery rocks affect the safety of access?

Even if the place looks totally safe, what are the **retreat options**? How *quickly* and *safely* can one beat a retreat? If one cannot retreat fast enough, is there a suitable rock close by that one could shelter *behind* in an emergency. Such rocks can be extremely useful in breaking a wave's force. It is wise to be aware of them in advance rather than having to hunt in an emergency.

▪ How safely and easily can one get to totally safe ground **carrying heavy awkward gear, and a big fish?**

▪ **What is the *potential* for waves to break over the rocks to be fished from?** The shape and height of rocks may facilitate, limit or preclude waves from breaking over the rocks. For instance, rocks which slope up towards the fisherman from the sea are potentially dangerous in that waves may run high up them, and pull the fisherman back down the slope into the sea. Assessing the potential for this is critical. Before fishing, watch all the scenarios in the area to familiarise yourself with wave action and sea behaviour against rocks. This will vary with tides and the angle and size of the swell. If unfamiliar with the area, err on the very cautious side. Keep far back. Wet rocks, especially if **smooth** and **weed-covered**, will be slippery. This can be *extremely treacherous*.

On rare occasions rocks are hollowed out under the angler in which case, if the rocks are high enough, waves will run in underneath and be harmlessly pushed back outwards. Although the impact of waves can be intimidating in these situations, such formations can be very protective – though the landing of big fish is then made more difficult, requiring a long gaff or alternatively and by far preferably, an easier landing site to which a fish can be led.

Vertical rock formations lie somewhere in between, and their safety or otherwise, like all cases, will depend on wave size, action, and the height of the rock above the sea – which will vary with the tide. Observation of wave action is the only way to assess them.

▪What will waves do to the actual fishing position? Is there any evidence of this, for instance wetness or seaweed growth on the rocks? The presence of seaweed, even dry seaweed, means the sea *definitely* reaches the spot, though absence of seaweed does not necessarily mean that it does not. It may do so only rarely – but just once at the wrong time could be once too often. The state of water in rock pools can be quite revealing too. Is this fresh or stagnant? Stagnant water generally indicates that waves relatively infrequently reach the spot, even at high tide, though it can also mean there has been a prolonged calm spell.

A previously un-fished venue needs to be watched *very* carefully for twenty minutes or more. An incoming (making) tide always needs to be treated with extra special care. **Note that over and above the fact that the sea level is rising on an incoming tide, waves will also be more forceful and aggressive.**

Always fish *well back* at first, until the fishing spot's idiosyncrasies can be established.

▪ **Are the rocks one would fish from formed in such a way that a wave breaking over them could wash one into the sea rather than back over rocks?** Being pushed backwards over rocks is bad enough, but if waves could wash one into the sea, this is potentially *highly dangerous*. If this could happen, such rocks need to be fished *extremely* carefully if at all and only by very experienced anglers. If you aren't very experienced in the sea's behaviour, then avoid the situation. It would be horribly embarrassing to have to be plucked from the sea by helicopter and displayed on national TV. Even worse, to be plucked out dead – which is more likely. Better to appear on TV with a big fish.

▪ While trends in wave patterns and behaviour are observable and may eventually be reasonably predictable, **the behaviour of every wave cannot be known in advance. Each and every wave could behave slightly (or considerably) differently from the trend.** *Every* wave needs to be watched. Apply the old advice '**never turn your back on the sea**' or if this is unavoidable, get a fishing buddy to watch the water for you.

▪ **How safe is the rocky terrain on which one will be standing, moving, casting, fighting and landing a fish?**

What is the footing and rock surface like, and are there any hand grips? Big fish pulling hard on strong line can be a dangerous mixture. If very heavy line is being used, a sharp knife in a sheath on the belt is essential, especially when targeting sharks. Work out a plan of movement for each stage of an anticipated fight with a fish. *Walk around the area before the real thing happens.*

▪ **How easily and safely can a fish be landed?** If the immediate vicinity is difficult or dangerous, can a fish be led to a safer, easier spot for landing? This is the author's first consideration for any new fishing spot.

Above: *Good weather for photography, bad weather for fishing. (Photo courtesy of Mike Thom.)*

2. **Clothing** (Relevant to safety)

▪ **Choose clothes that do not restrict the body's movement.**

▪ **Make sure there are no loose bits** (for example jacket pull-cords) that can get caught up in the reel handle when reeling in, or worse still, when playing a fish. Not only can this cause the loss of a fish, but in some situations it can cause a loss of balance which is potentially dangerous.

▪ **Choose footwear that doesn't slip.** Note that rough soles do *not* necessarily translate into non-slip soles on rocks. Some types of rubber that look as though they should grip well may do so on dry rock but be very slippery on wet rock, even with no wet seaweed. These are potentially treacherous. Test soles on *wet* rocks – you may be unpleasantly surprised but it could save your life. Very few materials will not slip on wet seaweed, and this can be even more treacherous. Although the author has not used them, rope soles are said to be one of the best options against the slipperiness of seaweed. Better still, keep off it. Watch where you are walking, every step. Note that oysters, barnacles and mussels on rocks are the opposite of seaweed, as they can be used to give an excellent non-slip grip.

The author often wears gumboots when rock fishing. These are cut down, but left high enough to protect the ankles. They are tough, protective, and in the author's experience generally have good non-slipping soles, even on wet rocks – though this must *never* be taken for granted in any footwear. It must be tested. Of course, getting a boot full of water is not much fun.

▪ The use of **life-jackets** is sometimes suggested, and one day may even be made compulsory. This sounds quite extreme; nevertheless it is a good idea for difficult terrain and deep water, provided the design and fit are good – not restricting on movement and not bulky enough to bump into the surrounds and cause a loss of balance. At least bruising to the body would be reduced in a fall. At age 63, the author now wears a good quality life jacket on the rocks. This is comfortable, and virtually non-restricting in movement.

▪ In addition to appropriate clothing, a **mobile phone,** water-proof, in a water-proof case, is highly recommended – *especially* for anyone fishing on their own (which is *not* recommended). Better still, a PLB (small personal locating beacon with GPS, in particular as used by yacht crew) is an excellent investment. These are small enough to fit into a pocket.

3.   The weather

▪ Fishing trips are rare and precious to most of us – or at least they feel that way. It can be a great disappointment to travel a long distance and walk a long way only to find last night's storm winds have created a nightmarishly rough sea. After all that *anticipation…* **Check the past few days' weather as well as forecasts before leaving on a fishing trip, and avoid disappointment or risk taking.**

Don't be tempted to take chances in dangerous circumstances – it just isn't worth it. Think about it: if we won every time, there'd be nothing to boast about. Let the sea win occasionally – you can boast about the incredible will-power it took to resist the temptation.

If fishing has to be done in bad weather, choose a venue which is **known to be safe** and forgo the riskier ones until things improve.

4.   Fitness, agility and surefootedness

These three physical attributes are critical for rock fishermen. Naturally not everyone can be a super-fit athlete, but fishermen must always be able to meet the demands of the terrain very comfortably.

5.   Familiarity

There is perhaps no single factor which can increase the safety of a venue more than familiarity by repeated experience. Knowing one's way around and knowing any nasty aspects of a venue, especially when fishing at night, make for easy, comfortable and safe fishing. Of course this must never lapse into over-confidence.

6.   Fishing buddies

• The author, as acknowledged, has fished far more in solitude than with companions. Nevertheless, *this is not recommended – it is in fact strongly discouraged.* It is undeniably far more sensible and safe to fish with companions. They provide extra eyes for watching waves, assistance in case of accidents, help with landing fish, etc. They may even help with your gear if you have to carry a big fish back, or confirm that the big one that got away *really was hooked and really was big!*

▪ If, like the author, you *will* fish on your own regardless of everyone's dire warnings, because that's what you were put on the planet for in the first place, then do it carefully and intelligently. *Don't take unnecessary risks.* No fish is worth it. Don't become part of the reason that laws get introduced to stop us from rock fishing. And tell people where you are headed, including potential changes of plan if appropriate.

As mentioned before, a PLB (personal locating beacon) could be a life-saver.

7.   Fishing off the rocks at night

This has to be the most dangerous aspect of rock fishing. Only *very experienced* anglers should do it, and only in very familiar or inherently safe spots. It is ABSOLUTELY FOOLHARDY for anyone but the most experienced. Only venues that have been fished in the daytime and are very well known and safe should be fished at night.

A good, bright, dependable headlamp is essential, along with a good, bright, dependable back-up torch. The back-up torch does not have to be a headlamp – it just needs to enable one to move safely if the headlamp fails.

A good moon can help enormously in seeing one's way around, but some fish seem to prefer dark moonless nights. If the sea is rough or exhibiting a behaviour that makes you feel uneasy, back off and wait for better conditions.

8.   Drinking alcohol on the rocks, or prior to fishing

DON'T!!!

Advice For The Novice Rock Angler

• Go only with someone very experienced, cautious and responsible on as many trips as possible.

• Choose protected areas and sheltered waters.

• Don't bite off more than you can chew – choose safe rocks with a flat easy area over which to retreat.

• Study the situation for yourself. What are the waves doing? Is the tide rising or falling? Take your time. Discuss your own assessment with your experienced companion.

• Only do it in the daytime until a *lot* of experience is gained.

•At first, fish as far back from the sea as possible.

•Familiarise yourself with the sea and its beautiful and fascinating, but potentially treacherous ways. Get to know wave patterns and behaviour. Get to know how rising or falling tides affect wave activity. Familiarise yourself with the times of, and differences between, the big full and new moon tides, and small neap tides in between. Get to know how very slippery wet rocks can be – and how *incredibly* slippery wet seaweed *is*.

▪ Talk to locals if possible, especially tackle shop owners – they will be able to give advice and also tell you if anyone has been washed off the rocks recently, and why.

▪ Treat the sea as the BOSS. (It *is* the boss!)

▪ Never turn your back on the boss.

▪ If in doubt about the conditions, give fishing a miss until they improve.

▪ Check through the preceding points, and apply the advice given there.

Chapter 13

Some Considerations And Methods That Could Help To Ensure That Big Fish Are Landed Successfully

1.   The Venue - Where And How Can A Fish Be Landed?

After safety, this is the single most important aspect of any rocky fishing spot, and landing the fish is the greatest challenge. Unfortunately some of the most beautiful and potentially productive fishing spots cannot be fished at all because fish simply cannot be landed there. This can be very frustrating, but at least it creates a natural sanctuary for fish.

The following should be assessed before fishing commences:

▪ Where can the fight (from beginning to end) be conducted from? Is the rock slippery? How easy will it be to maintain balance during a strong fight? Are there places in the rock to hold onto? If you fall, where do you fall to?

▪ Is there more than one option in landing sites? (Unfortunately there is far more often *no* good landing site than having a choice of two.)

▪ Is there a sandy beach situated nearby and would it be possible to lead a fish to it for landing? This is a wonderful option if available, and safely and comfortably accessible.

▪ Is there anywhere such as a gully or inlet amongst the rocks that the fish can be led to, which is sheltered and offers access for gaffing or even hand access? Wave action in the area must be observed thoroughly, long before the place needs to be used for landing the first fish.

At Black Rock near Mbolompo on the Wild Coast, shown below as an example, big fish tend to wash from right to left with the prevailing current. This can be encouraged while the fish is still far out in the clear rock-free water by keeping tension on the line but not retrieving line unless necessary to maintain the tension. If the fish is brought too close too soon there is an outcrop of rock on the left corner (not visible in the picture) which can be troublesome to get a fish past. Once past this point, pressure must be put on the fish to get it out of the current and into the sheltered bay and inlet on the left side of the rock – a superb landing site. If it washes too far it may become difficult or impossible to pull back against the wash, and a very big fish may end up in the rocks on the far left (out of view in the photo). The right hand side of the main rock is not conducive to landing a big fish.

Every rocky spot will have positive and negative attributes such as these; some simple, some complex. Even sandy beaches can have features which make landing easier or more difficult, and encouraging large fish to move a distance (if they will) can sometimes make things easier, but by and large it is infinitely easier to land fish off a sandy beach than from the rocks.

Right: *The beautiful Black Rock north of Mbolompo Point, Wild Coast, South Africa. Home to big denizens, yet quite user friendly if the right strategies are used.*

• Are there sloping rocks up which a fish could be progressively lifted using a series of waves until it can be safely reached by hand or gaff? The rocks must be watched to see how waves behave when they hit them – sloping rocks can be as treacherous as they can be useful. Watch for waves running up them relative to where it would be necessary to stand to land the fish, noting smooth slippery surfaces and especially seaweed. Conversely, barnacle, oyster and mussel growth can provide excellent grip.

▪ Are there any obstacles in the way of leading a fish to the landing spot? For example, is there evidence of rocky outcrops at the edge, underwater or exposed, around which a fish may have to be guided – usually against its will? Such rocks can be *very* problematic, especially if they are encrusted with line-cutting rock life.

▪ Is there a strong side-wash? Do the wave action and currents move in the required direction to get the fish to the landing spot, or do waves push in the opposite direction? A strong current pulling against a big fish can make it difficult or impossible to get the fish to go where it needs to go. Conversely, one can sometimes position oneself so as to take advantage of wave action or currents.

2.   Playing the fish

Some universal principles apply here, but before getting to these let us look at two different situations. First there is the scenario of having plenty of line, and a large obstacle-free area (no rocks or other obstructions) in which to play the fish, and in which case the fish can be allowed to have its head to some degree. This makes for a relatively relaxed fight. It is fine to allow the fish to run against a reasonably hard but safe level of drag in these circumstances, while still monitoring line reserves. The fish will tire itself in the process until it can be turned.

On the other hand, if line is limited, the fish big and powerful, or the area is foul, as much pressure as possible will be needed to prevent it from stripping the reel or cutting itself free. The worst-case scenario in this situation is 'hold the fish or lose it'. Repeated hard pumping (with or without retrieving line), which is a similar movement to striking, but slower, smoother and longer, without jerking can help to stop, hold or turn the fish, as these make manoeuvring difficult for it. Excessively hard and jerky strikes are risky as the strain on the line peaks very high in these circumstances and may push the line over its limit.

Above: *Good looking water at 1770, Queensland, Australia, but challenging due to the large exposed rocks in front which may cause problems while playing a fish. Surface-fighting species such as mackerel are easier in these circumstances, but deeper fighters such as kingfish and trevally will be more difficult to land.*

Very importantly, as soon as the fish has turned, it is wise to reduce the drag's tension to a safer level; that is, to a level at which it can take line without breaking it if it decides to run, but which is still hard enough to keep pressure on the fish and enable line to be retrieved. The angler needs to be prepared for sudden runs any time after the fish has been turned. These subsequent runs are rarely as powerful as the initial run, though big sharks and occasionally some fish can produce exceptions to this rule.

In either of the above circumstances, the moment the fish stops or is turned, focus must shift to retrieving line, urgently if this has been badly depleted. Because movements which can be felt by the fish can easily trigger a new run, while retrieving line every effort should be made to work smoothly, especially if only a little line remains on the spool. This is done by raising the rod, carefully and slowly pulling back line, and winding smoothly as the rod is lowered again, attempting to keep a reasonably constant and even tension. The runs are in any case likely to occur again as the fish approaches shallower water or the edge of the rocks or beach, but by this time there should be line to spare. As always, the drag must be set to allow line to be taken in the event of a run.

The pull-by-lifting-the-rod-upwards and winding-as-the-rod-is-lowered action is continued, releasing line if necessary, though holding as hard as is safe – or as hard as possible if the fish appears to be making a dash for rocks. The longer the fight continues, the less likely it is that the fish will produce a long run. Note that the reel should never be used alone to winch a fish in as this is extremely hard on the reel and may cause damage or shorten its lifespan.

When fishing from the beach, apart from being stripped, fish-losing threats are generally much reduced. One of the most useful means for helping to control a first run which threatens to strip the reel, and to turn the tables to enable a recovery of line without scaring the fish into extending its run, is to walk carefully backwards over the sand if space permits once the fish has been turned, instead of attempting recovery by winding the line immediately back on the reel. This enables line to be retrieved without any pumping movement to the line, which if detected, can *very* easily scare the fish into an extended and potentially terminal run.

Once ten or twenty paces have been walked, this line can be retrieved by winding as one walks back towards the sea's edge. Even this will sometimes trigger a run, but at least the angler can now accommodate this by walking forwards, simultaneously attempting to minimize the extent of the fresh run by maintaining maximum possible pressure, always with the rod upright or nearly upright to buffer any sudden lunges by the fish. As always the drag must be set low enough to allow line to be taken off well before its breaking strain is reached.

This strategy can be repeated until the threat of being stripped is well and truly over. Thereafter the same tactics can be employed as described above until the fish can be landed, which provided patience is exercised, is a relatively simple matter on a beach.

3.   Landing the fish

Once the fish has been turned and line retrieval has commenced, thoughts need to turn to landing. A position should already have been decided upon, and it is now a matter of persuading the fish to go where needed. This usually requires a combination of gentle and strong persuasion. If this is achievable it does not pay to bring a big fish too close to the rocks before it is lined up with the landing point, as it can be extremely difficult to get fish to move in a desired direction once they reach the edge. Furthermore, in doing so it is very easy to foul a line when the fish is close, and even if it doesn't decide to make a dash for some rocky ledge it can be difficult or impossible to get it to move straight out again into clear water. If a fish can safely be fought until it tires before approaching the rocks, this is normally the best option but is not always possible.

With slower-moving fish it is often possible to encourage them to 'tend towards' the desired spot, for example by pulling on the line to increase their speed when they are facing and moving in the right direction. This is largely done by feel, and situations will vary, but experience slowly reveals tendencies by different species which can be exploited. A long rod helps in directing the fish once it is at close quarters.

When a fish close by is moving in the right direction, the pull on the rod should be steady – jerks may prompt the fish to run, causing valuable ground to be lost. If the fish still makes attempts to run as it tires and approaches, as they very often do, careful pressure can be applied every time it runs so that the distances achieved each time will decrease, and gains will increase – but always with the drag set such that the line will be released well before the breaking strain of the line is reached.

Bear in mind that as the distance between fish and angler decreases there is less stretch available in the line. If the drag is too tight, there is an *increasing* possibility of the line snapping if the fish lunges when the drag has not been progressively loosened. This is critical. Constant awareness of drag tension during the entire fight is of paramount importance. Furthermore, the rod should *never* be allowed to point directly at the fish because the 'give' provided by the flexing of the rod is then lost when it may be most needed.

As the fish nears the landing point, especially if it is to be landed on the rocks, attention must be turned to the wave action, and how this can best be used to manoeuvre or lift the fish to within reach. The fish is eventually encouraged to the surface with maximum safe pressure if necessary, rather than have it washed irretrievably past the landing point. Considerable but carefully applied pressure may be needed at the last minute. If the fish is well tired, it should be possible to hold it at the surface reasonably easily until the right wave or waves arrive. Once at the surface, the fish is carefully manoeuvred progressively towards and then onto the landing point with one or more swells. On each occasion the fish will need to be carefully held against being pulled back by the now returning water if it is being landed on a slope. This can take considerable pressure and skill if the fish is large. The drag must have been prepared in advance to allow the fish to slide back without the line breaking if it can't be held. It is better to have it slide back than have the line break. Many fish are lost by the line breaking in these circumstances. If the fish slips back, the procedure then has to be repeated. In this late stage of the fight, and earlier if necessary, the fingers can be used to apply pressure to the line or spool (depending on the type of reel) to increase or decrease the resistance required for line to be released. This reduces the need to work with the drag itself, and is quicker and easier to action.

The fish is progressively encouraged inwards/upwards until a 'resting place' can be found in or on which it can be deposited, such as a pool or crack in the rocks from which it can be safely retrieved by hand or gaffed, and from which waves will not easily wash it back down.

Rock formations, slopes, waves, currents and the species of fish all play a role in the best landing techniques, and vary from occasion to occasion, so although principles apply, each case will be different.

4.   Gaffing the fish

If gaffing is required and the fish can't be brought to an easy access point, this can be difficult and potentially very dangerous. Fishermen have lost their lives while attempting to gaff other people's fish, or even their own. Every possible effort should be made to bring the fish to the best possible access, even if this takes time. It is *always* the responsibility of the angler to position the fish in the safest and easiest position possible for gaffing. Obviously rocky purchase by the gaffer needs to be substantial and wave action must be monitored extremely closely. *No one should ever have to take dangerous risks for someone else's fish.*

It is usually far easier to get the gaff hook to penetrate by going under the fish with the gaff hook pointing upwards. Furthermore it is far more difficult to position the gaff and set the hook in the fish from above, with the hook pointing down. In this position the gaff hook will more easily slip off the fish rather than penetrating. If the gaff hook is under water, it can be difficult to ensure that the hook is facing upwards. It is helpful to mark the upper side of the gaff handle clearly in white (especially for night gaffing) to make this easily visible.

The gaffer should be encouraged by the angler himself not to take risks, as it is easy to get carried away with the action. Naturally the angler, and any observers, must *constantly advise the gaffer of the behaviour of the sea* as he will be focussed on gaffing.

The gaffer must approach the fish for gaffing carefully and with thought – it is *extremely* easy to break a tight line with a gaff. And this is an exceptionally fast way to lose fish and angling friends. All too often one sees gaffers slashing wildly at fish. This is very bad practice.

If the fish is to be released, if achievable it is best hooked carefully through the lower jaw if it cannot be lifted

Left: *Dealing with the stress of poor catches! Note the large baked enamel mug – perfect for the purpose, using 'firewater' left over from negotiations with indunas. The rope was incidental – it never gets that bad. There's always tomorrow.*

by hand. Flying gaffs are appropriate for some venues, but have rarely been used by the author.

To finish off this chapter, let me say that sometimes despite one's very best efforts, dedication and hours of work in seemingly perfect conditions, the fish just won't oblige. Time then to pack it in, go home or back to camp and console oneself with a hard earned drink!

Chapter 14

A Final Few Words

I don't think many people read epilogues, so I'm making this chapter 14. Furthermore, had it been an epilogue, there would have been thirteen chapters in this book. *Thirteen* chapters in a book on rock-fishing? NO WAY! So Chapter 14 it is.

When Mike Thom heard that I was writing a book on fishing (including its close relative, humour), he wrote to me, using my nickname:

22 October 2006

Dear Kob,

I was there in the incredible 70s and 80s and can remember not only Mbolompo but all the unbelievable incidents as if it was yesterday. I can even hear the rocks rolling in the gully and smell the sea. Mcwasa Point and Mbolompo – the words conjure up a magic that only someone who has been there can understand. What fond memories! Pure nostalgia.

I wonder how someone who has never been there would read the same script. How could they understand? Well my dear friend, when you get to that part of the story you will have to pull some magic out of the hat, which I'm sure you can. You know when this global warming brings on the next Ice Age and mankind retreats back to the Stone Age and then re-emerges as civilized, maybe twenty million years from now, he might find a new world much like the ancients once knew.

If the newly civilized man then went down to the sea and threw a line into that fresh, recharged ocean he might just sense that intense anticipation and excitement that you and I once felt at Mbolompo. What monsters might there be? What awesome tug might he feel not only on his line but on the strings of his heart? I know you know the feeling.

Best wishes

Bones.

Thanks for that Mike, and thanks for helping to make the memories. Maybe one day when another heaven and another earth come to pass we may again find ourselves clambering down hills, over rocks and through marshy streams, straining our eyes in the first light of the day to find out how the sea is behaving at the 'Sacred Fishing Spot'…

*** The End ***